Confessions of a Band Geek Mom

By

Stacy Dymalski

The stories in this book are based upon true events. However, in some cases the names, places, and times in history have been changed (mainly so the people depicted can deny it was them, in case they don't want to own up).

2011 Saffire Press Trade Paperback Edition

Library of Congress Cataloging-in-Publication
Dymalski, Stacy
Confessions of a Band Geek Mom
ISBN 978-0-615-47499-1

Printed in the United States of America

Book cover by Michelle Rayner of Cosmic Design
cosmicdesignllc.com

To my sons, Derrick and Quinn.

You're the best sanity check any parent could have.

Mom

To the people and town of Park City.

If it takes a village to raise a child, I'm so glad my sons were lucky enough to grow up in your kitchens, classrooms, and backyards.

S.D.

Other books by Stacy Dymalski

The Vixen Chronicles

DUI: Dating Under the Influence of Some Very Bad Men

(cowritten with Brandy Pinkerman Janke)

About the Author

Stacy Dymalski is a freelance writer, filmmaker and stand-up comic. Her screen credits include cowriter (with Zack Van Eyck)/director of the feature film *Jupiter Landing* and writer/director of the web sitcom series *Hagnet*. She also blogs career advice for the educational websites *Careers and Classes* and *Yellow Brick Road*. You can follow her on Twitter at @StacyWriteNow and keep up with her on her website*.

She lives in Park City, Utah, with her husband and two sons.

*Stacy's website:
http://web.me.com/stacy_dymalski/Writer/Welcome.html

Confessions of a Band Geek Mom

Contents

Acknowledgments

As a mom you meet so many people on a daily basis who help out in unexpected ways that it's hard to keep track of them all. Even in those rare moments when you have a nanosecond of free time, and you find yourself reflecting on your day, week, month or year, these angels are hard to recall because they just swoop in as needed and then leave. For example, there's the person at the grocery store who helps you pick up the tower of cereal boxes your child toppled; the parent at the cooperative preschool who stays after school with your kid because you were late to pick-up; the moms in your playgroup who don't judge you if you snap at your little one on a bad day; the third-grade teacher who tutors your son on her own time so he won't fall behind in reading.

To all these and others (too many to mention) I say,

"Thank you." Before I had kids I was kind of a loner, and I never knew how much I'd end up depending on you all for support. I'm fortunate to live in a community that collectively cares about its youth, and as you'll see when you read this book, it was just a fluke that I ended up here once the babies came along. I'm not sure what I did to be so lucky.

I'd also like to thank my writing chums, Dee Macaluso, Annette Velarde, and Lynn Ware for reading these stories, offering input, providing edits, and listening to me whine when the going got tough. Your opinions are invaluable and I'm not sure I could have put this book together without you.

To Lyn Eckels, thank you so much for lending me your "editor's eyes." Your talent allows me to concentrate on my thoughts and feelings instead of the proper placement of a hyphen. You are a wonderful editor and an even better friend. Thank you so much for reading my book, giving meaningful feedback, and not laughing at my poor spelling.

To Michelle Rayner, who created this beautiful book cover, you are an artistic goddess. I can't thank you enough for devoting your valuable time and talent to my little project. You're a wonderful example of one of those "angels" who was there when needed.

And finally, thank you to my husband and two sons, especially my sons, for giving me adventures to write about. My life changed dramatically once you kids came along, but now that I'm over halfway through your childhoods (you're in tenth and seventh grades as I write this) I see it was definitely for the better. I have added precious layers to my soul that never would've existed without you.

– Stacy Dymalski

Preface: The Summer Vacation I'll Tell My Grandkids About

When I was 11 years old, I went to work with my dad. This may not seem like such a big deal, except that my parents were divorced, so I hardly ever got to see my father. Plus, he was an investigative reporter for the *Oakland Tribune*, and as such he was routinely sent out to cover the underbelly of the Bay Area, like suspected mob activities, car bombings, gang violence, and even the Patty Hearst kidnapping (which came to his attention by way of a middle-of-the-night phone call the night she was taken—I suspect he knew before the local police).

My limited time with my dad was precious. And even though he was young and ambitious, working on a career he had dreamt of his whole life, he was determined to be an attentive father when I was around. He deserved an A for effort, but even as a child I knew, despite his genuine attempts, his overall parenting skills needed to be graded on a curve.

The last of a dying breed of hard-boiled reporters, my dad loved piecing together loose ends to find a story that menacing characters would kill to keep out of print. My mother suspected he hung out with unsavory types, which is one of the reasons why she didn't like me visiting him. But he persisted, and so did I. Eventually my dad and I got to know each other better, and as a result realized we were spilt from the same bottle of ink. This revelation gave him the very "unparental" notion that he should take me to work so he could share with me his love of nosing around in other people's business. And since I was a feisty little girl who felt life's adventures should start no later than age 11, I jumped at the chance to be his sidekick. My mother, who was 700 miles away, would absolutely have put her foot down (probably on his neck) had she known.

My first day, I walked into the bullpen of the *Trib* to the deafening sound of the *tap, tap, tap* of manual typewriters, like some manic Morse Code that only truly dedicated writers could understand. These were the pre-computer, pre-Internet days when the paper never closed, which meant some of the reporters had been there all night, making phone calls, checking facts, resisting sleep just to make the morning edition. They all smoked like incinerators, so a thick, white fog dangled over the room. I probably lost five years off my life just breathing an hour's worth of that air.

But even knowing that now I don't care, because the excitement in that place was as magnetic as static electricity: snitches spilling their guts for a pack of smokes, high-strung editors foaming at the mouth, copy boys running stories to press, my dad and I going on an interview, reporters stressing over deadlines, and in some cases standing up to death threats. To me it was a bigger adventure than even Mark Twain could imagine. The sense of urgency at the *Trib* made everything else seem trivial. In retrospect, it felt like a hospital emergency room, but instead of doctors saving lives it was reporters *changing* lives, some for the better, some for the worse, but in either case they were responsible for getting the story out to the public, regardless of the risks and without the cloud of judgment. *I thought that was so cool!*

Looking back I realize those summers with my dad weren't what you'd consider normal family vacations. In fact, my dad and I never had the opportunity to go on one of those traditional family trips that parents think they have to give their kids in order to be good parents. We never went to Disneyland, or the beach, or camping, or to some coveted destination like Hawaii. Yet, he gave me chapters for my life that no kid could ever find at a theme park.

Which made me think about my own kids and what kind

of memories I'm making for them. I would love to be able to afford to take my kids to Europe to see the Louvre, Big Ben, Madrid, the fjords, and anything else that appears on the homepage of a glossy AAA travel website. But that's just not in the cards for us. However, given my experience with my own unconventional childhood, I know you don't have to always do the regular family stuff in order to make a lasting impression on your kids. Sometimes being a little *irregular* sparks a fonder memory.

So even if you can afford to take your kids scuba diving on the Great Barrier Reef or get them floor seats at a Lakers game, maybe it'd be worth it to take a step back first and think about what impressed you when you were a kid. Chances are you were dazzled when your dad asked you to join him on one of his weekly bowling nights. Or when your mom took you school shopping and then out to dinner, just the two of you. Or when you all went on a family bike ride together. Ironically, the stories I'll tell my grandkids about my childhood won't be the ones where my parents forked out a boatload of cash. They'll be the ones that allowed me a glimpse into who my parents really were. Just like with my dad at the *Trib*.

After witnessing my dad's passion for journalism, I understood, even then, why it prevented him from settling down to a life of parent-teacher conferences and nightly family dinners. He chose a different path. And that's okay, because then he chose to share that path with me. Thankfully, he was not the dad in *Father Knows Best*, because his tendency to march counter to formation not only led to some of the best recollections of my childhood, it taught me how to make some great memories for my own kids.

The Party's Over (Or Is It?)

Back when America didn't know it's entire financial institution was a house of straw built on a pile of quicksand, I lived in a sleepy little town about a mile inland from San Diego County's Moonlight Beach. I owned a nice home with my husband and made lots of money working as a big talker.

It was the early '90s so unbeknownst to us Wall Street and the banking industry were busy perfecting their little derivative magic trick—the one where the big reveal would be the eventual meltdown of both the financial and housing markets some 18 years later. But at the time the illusion made us believe prosperity was attainable even to the dumbest of chumps, and that poverty was about as fashionable as a beauty queen with B.O. and bucked teeth. As a result big businesses (thought they) had more money than they knew what to do with, and I quickly figured out that they liked to spend it on entertainers disguised as technical consultants.

Armed with a math degree from University of California, Berkeley, and the ability to speak cleverly in front of large crowds without wetting my pants, I morphed into a technical trainer and keynote speaker for high-profile clients such as Hewlett Packard, IBM, and Adobe. Even though I knew my stuff when it came to pontificating on the wonders of bits, bytes, baud, and BIOS, there was no denying these folks got quite a show when I worked the room.

But it was a sanitized (and limited) version of how I saw the world, so to accommodate my quirky sense of humor I also regularly performed stand-up in clubs all around the country, but mainly in Southern California. I perfected my shtick at The Comedy Store, The Improv, The Ice House, and countless trendy, little coffee houses and bars that dotted the coast between Hollywood and La Jolla. I was even a finalist in the 1991 Southern California Comedy Competition, which was taped for some obscure cable channel that was supposedly nipping at the heals of Comedy Central. Out of the 10 finalists there were only three women, of which I was one. Comedy was (and still is) a male-dominated field, as was technology, and at the time I was holding my own in both.

But because the guys who invented YouTube and Twitter were still in diapers, I actually had to leave my house in order to find an audience, so I traveled a lot on business and usually went first class. Back then airlines doled out free first-class upgrades to frequent flyers the way they now hand out those cheap, stale peanuts—sparingly, but they'd give them up if you asked.

Not one to miss an opportunity to maximize my travel expenses, I always booked myself into the local comedy clubs whenever I showed up in a new city as a technical trainer. By day I'd rattle on to entire roomfuls of corporate propeller-heads about how desktop publishing (which was brand-spanking new at the time) was going to solve all our problems and create a paperless society of world peace (or some such nonsense), and then at night I'd hit the local comedy clubs where I'd talk about what it was like to have small breasts in a high school that seemed to spawn nothing but Pamela Anderson clones. (Typical inscription in any girl's yearbook at my high school *except* mine: "Dear Desiree, Thanks for the mammaries," or "To Karen, Your cups runneth over." Not the wittiest of prose, but it was enough to give me a complex deep enough to share with 200 drunken strangers nightly in clubs that smelled like a cross between some beach bum's sweaty tank top and stale Bud Light.)

Even though I wasn't well-known outside of Southern California (okay, fine, I wasn't even *that* well-known within Southern California) the club owners in these obscure little towns would always let me get up onstage because I was an L.A. comic for whom they didn't have to pay travel expenses. I'd do my two sets, get paid, and then leave. Once in a while they'd invite me back, but only if I happened to be passing through again. I guess I was good enough for a return engagement, but not good enough to spring for gas money.

Yes, by golly, life was really, really good back then. One. Big. Lucrative. Party. And even though I rarely went to bed before 2:00 a.m., I still always looked well-rested because I slept in late everyday. Plus, I laughed for a living and got all the free drinks I wanted. It was the kind of existence in which one assumes happy hour is part of everyone's daily commute no matter where the road goes.

This totally delusional impression of reality went on for several years, until finally one day I turned to my husband and said, "Honey, do you think we're missing something here?"

"Nope," he quickly answered. "Could you pass the caviar, please?"

"Oh. Sure. Right after I open another bottle of wine." I paused to consider my original question. "You know, we've kind of done everything, been everywhere, bought lots of stuff. Don't you ever wonder what's next?"

"What do you mean?"

"I don't know. Maybe… have some kids?"

I could tell by his Cabernet spit take and the sour look on his face that he wasn't too keen on that idea. We always knew we wanted to have kids *someday*, and even though we'd been married for seven years by this time, we just weren't sure when that day would come.

But I was getting close.

So to take my mind off Diaper Genies and breast pumps my husband suggested we buy a house in Park City, Utah, and split our time between Southern California and that incredible Wasatch powder. We did (because why the hell not?), and to my surprise we became so enamored with shoveling snow (hey, we were beach people, what did we know?) that we eventually sold our house in Encinitas and cashed out of California all together. I'm not sure what we were thinking, but at the time it somehow made sense. I still traveled, and did comedy, but now my husband suddenly had enough free time to get chummy with all the local ski lift operators and study up on how to get around Utah's funky liquor laws.

We were having so much fun traveling, skiing, laughing, partying, making money, and buying tons of stuff we didn't need that any thought of ever having children suddenly drained out of my head faster than vodka pouring from a Martini shaker.

That's when I got pregnant.

Cue the needle scratch across a record; the screeching of brakes; the sound of glass shattering; a saxophone blowing "wah, wah, wahhhh." Actually, it wasn't a total surprise. We'd been half-heartedly, sort of, kind of, but not really, trying to have a baby for about a year. But every month the stick refused to turn blue. So to protect myself from further disappointment I just gave up and assumed my womb was as barren as Park City's Jupiter Bowl in the middle of January.

Which, by the way, really irritated me on a whole other level (my barren womb, that is, not Park City's Jupiter Bowl) given that NOW (at this late point in my life) I find out I wasted all that money all those years on birth control? Not to mention the panic I endured any time I happened to be *late*. All that stress, and now you're telling me I can't even get pregnant? That does it, I thought at the time. I'm buying a water-ski boat and calling it good.

But we never got around to that ski boat because finally the stick did turn blue. And so did my husband's face after I told him we were having a baby. It's not that he didn't *want* children. Turns out he was just *afraid* to have them. Apparently all the talks we'd had previously about one day spawning a family was, um, well, just talk. You see *discussing* a baby and actually *having* one are two different things altogether. Reality has a way of sobering you up. It'd been just the two of us for so long that our egocentric lifestyle (and steady stream of bountiful income) had become routine. And now he was worried that it would all change when a baby entered the picture.

As the compassionate wife, I thought he was just being stupid.

We were in our mid thirties and old enough to know better than to let something as small as a baby alter who we were. I refused to be one of those weak, whiny parents who wasn't smart enough to schedule Gymboree play dates around regular massages and winetasting parties.

I told my husband we'd still ski 40 days a year, travel, and spend money on ourselves like we had an endless supply, because I'd still work as a stand-up and technical trainer (after, of course, a respectable six weeks off to get to know Junior). Never mind that I had to travel all over the country to do it, we'd just take the little blob with us and set him up in one of those baby bucket car seat thingies where he'd sleep on command or entertain himself quietly by staring at a black-and-white cardboard face while listening to his Mozart headset. I mean really, how hard could it be to change a Prada satchel into a diaper bag? Just stick some Huggies in the darn thing and *voilà*, you've got yourself a designer carrier for baby's nappies. Yes, I'd already done my homework, so by now I was an expert on parenting, with an above-average expertise in babies.

Good lord, what a pretentious horse's ass I was.

In retrospect my husband had every right to be worried. No matter what you think about having a baby, no matter how many books you read, how many experts you listen to, or how much advice you take from parents who've gone before you, you have no idea what you're in for until you do it. And that's both the beauty and the curse of having children. It's a wild ride on a runaway train without a seat belt.

For me it turned out to be nothing like I'd expected, starting with the moment I laid eyes on my new little son (who turned out to be not so little at roughly nine pounds— also unexpected). The thought of leaving him to go on the road after our first six weeks together broke my heart. I did try for a whole year after he was born to continue working. But to make it easier on *me* I took him and his father along when I had to leave. We looked like some sort of trailer-trash, traveling circus, what with the car seat, the stroller, the portable crib, the baby swing, the breast pump, the multiple diaper bags, and several rolling suitcases that contained nothing but disposable diapers and onesies. We'd stand at the luggage carousel collecting bag after bag as they spewed out of the bowels of the airport. It was like watching those endless scarves come out of a magician's sleeve.

After a year I couldn't take it anymore. I quit my job cold turkey to stay home and happily wallow in spit-up and baby poop. My husband was worried we couldn't live off his income alone, and he was right. We couldn't keep up our old lifestyle, but fortunately we were both too exhausted on a daily basis from taking care of the baby to go out and do the things we used to do. So instead we stayed in, became hermits (which, by the way, saves a lot of money), and my husband telecommuted from home while I gained weight and let my leg and armpit hair grow. (Lovely.) I guess our financial situation sort of took care of itself.

Eventually my designer wardrobe began to dwindle. Donna Karan jeans gave way to sweat pants, my acrylic manicure wore off for good, and my most frequent form of exercise was lifting my son in and out of his highchair. But I didn't care because I actually felt centered for the first time in my life. I can't say I was jump-for-joy happy every day, but the highs were so cool that they far outweighed the occasional lows.

Within two years I was pregnant again. Proof that your memory is the ultimate deceiver when you rely on it to recall stressful events in your life—like childbirth.

On a sunny August day in 1998 I went to Park City's City Park to watch my three-year-old play with the other townie toddlers. (In a city of barely 5,000 residents at the time, all the toddlers pretty much knew each other.) My second son was due in October, so I was uncomfortable from the bloated effects of my third trimester. As I rested on a park bench feeling like my bulbous body was stuffed into a kielbasa skin that was about six sizes too small, an attractive older woman sat down next to me. "Excuse me," she said. "Did you used to do comedy in San Diego?"

I looked at her incredulously. I didn't know whether to be flattered or insulted that she recognized me. I wasn't exactly looking my best. "Uh, yeah," I confessed. "But now I'm doing other things." I looked at my son on the swings. He was having a blast—as my feet swelled by the second.

"The night I saw you we took my girlfriend to the Comedy Store for her bachelorette party," she reminisced. "It was her third marriage and none of us expected it to last, so we were pretty crazy. But you were into it; you were so funny. God, that was a wild night." I honestly couldn't remember which night she was talking about because back then they were all wild.

"Yeah, well, as you can see, the party's over," I said a little too pitifully while patting my gargantuan belly.

"Oh, I don't know," she countered, as she graciously pulled her Igloo cooler over to elevate my puffy feet (which by now looked like two giant eggplants). "From where I'm sitting, I'd say the party's just getting started."

Turns out she was absolutely right.

A Year in a Life

A year after my first son was born, I felt compelled to throw the requisite, big hoo-ha, Mardi Gras-ish, quinceanera-for-tots-type, baby bar mitzvah-style, professionally-catered one-year-old birthday party. Unfortunately, there wasn't anyone around at the time with a piñata bat to knock some sense into me.

Let me share something with you they don't tell you when you take your little miracle home from the hospital. The evolution of the children's birthday party is not unlike a twelve-step recovery program. In other words, it takes you (the parent) 12 years to realize that the best kids' parties involve nothing more than a frozen pizza, a carton of Haagen-Dazs, and some pitted black olives for the little darlings to stick on their fingers (but be sure to get the extra large ones so they can't stick them up their noses—nothing ruins a party faster than a trip to the emergency room with a kid that isn't yours).

Even though you'll throw lots of kids' parties in your child's lifetime, rest assured the first one will absolutely be the most ridiculous. If you're already picturing clowns, pony rides, climbing walls, magicians, out-of-town guests, and a cast of thousands for your one-year-old's party, you need to get to a support group right away. Listen as the experts explain how 20 minutes after the extravaganza begins Junior will become so overwhelmed he'll pitch a fit, which includes these lovely events unfolding in the following order:

1)   Banging his head on the ground in full view of Grandma's judgmental eyes.

2)   Throwing up the gourmet carrot cake that some artisan painstakingly crafted into the shape of SpongeBob SquarePants.

3)   Falling asleep in a sugar coma that'll last at least 12 hours (which will give you plenty of time to unwrap the mountains of large, colored plastic objects that eventually take over your house like prairie dogs in heat).

I speak from experience. I'm a recovering party-aholic myself. For my eldest son's first birthday, I stayed up the entire night before papier-mâché-ing a piñata (because, you know, the store-bought ones weren't good enough), only to watch in horror the next day as it was pummeled into a gleeful pulp by 15 kids in search of the bite-sized Snickers in a sea of cheap taffy and sour balls. The pictures of my shock don't do me justice. Rest assured, I wanted to hurt someone.

Then, of course, I had to make a cake (because, you know, the store-bought ones weren't good enough). Never mind that the only things I had ever baked at high altitude (I live at 7,000 feet) were cookies, all of which eventually found useful lives as hockey pucks and hammers. That's the year I learned how to lie convincingly. I passed off my undercooked-in-the-center birthday cake as a pudding pie. I'm sure they all believed me when I kept saying, "Uh yeah, you're supposed to eat it with a spoon—or a straw."

The irony of all this is that a child's first birthday party is not for the child at all—it's for the parents, grandparents, aunts, uncles, cousins; you know, that cast of thousands I mentioned earlier. Trust me, even though your child is the genius you always knew existed somewhere in your family tree (on your side, of course), Junior will not remember his first birthday party.

That's why I've always thought that for at least the first five years of a child's life (if not longer), the *mom* should be the one who is honored on her child's birthday, with a big party for *her*, at which *she* gets all the presents, preferably things like pedicures and massages. I mean, come on, it's only fair! *She's* the one who had to retain water like a cistern in a hurricane for 40 weeks (which is actually 10 months, so I don't know where they get that nine-month pregnancy nonsense). *She's* the one who had to give up alcohol and coffee during one the biggest (and most stressful) hormonal changes of her life (undoubtedly causing her dear, sweet, non-childbearing husband to drink more—in front of her, no doubt). And *she's* the one who forever gets to wear those eternal badges of maternal honor—emaciated, shrunken boobs (that have fully embraced gravity) and a saggy butt that's doing it's best to meet and greet the backs of her thighs. Oh yeah, *that's* a great look.

So save yourself a lot of grief. When your baby's one-year mark rolls around, stick a candle in a cupcake, take some video, and call it a day. Then after Junior goes to bed, *turn off* the camera, invite your best pals over, and spend the evening letting everyone toast you and your overworked uterus with Cadillac Margaritas. Later in life, when your child asks about his first birthday, you can dazzle your precious darling with home movies that would make Spielberg proud. Then while wistfully reminiscing you can honestly say, "Yes, sweetheart, your first birthday was one of the best parties of my life."

The Art of Using Scissors
(Blood and Gore, Part 1)

I've been using scissors for decades. My first memory of scissors was when I cut my cousin's hair with pinking shears when we were toddlers. My grandma wasn't happy (she was supposed to be watching us), but it really wasn't my fault. Since I had used packing tape to style my cousin's hair (we couldn't find barrettes) I had no choice but to perform surgery on her blond tresses. Unfortunately, I had to cut her hair rather short, which turned out to be a nonissue. They had to shave her head anyway when the doctor stitched up her scalp due to the big gash I had inflicted on top of her head. I was frantically trying to get rid of that darn tape before any adult could figure out what we were doing. That's also when I learned that even the smallest head wound hemorrhages like a severed limb. Nothing gets adults riled up more quickly than a bald, screaming child with blood spewing down her face and her precocious cousin chasing after her with scissors in one hand and a detached golden braid in the other. Who knew? I was only three.

As an adult, I feel I'm quite the expert with scissors. So imagine my bewilderment when a four-year-old at my son's preschool told me, "You're not doing it right," as I was cutting out the outline of my hand drawn on a brown grocery bag to make the requisite Thanksgiving paper turkey.

"What do you mean, I'm not doing it right?" I shot back.

"This is preschool," she retorted. "We don't hold scissors *like that.*"

"Like what?" I was now fully engaged in an argument I could never win.

The unabashed tot took the scissors and showed me how to cut paper. At this point I could see where she was coming from. I *was* holding the scissors wrong (upside down, as a matter of fact), but it worked for me. My mother is left-handed, and even though I'm right-handed, I do a lot of things backwards (or at least what is considered backwards) because my mother taught me that way.

"Don't you think it's kind of fun to be different?" I asked, trying to defend myself.

The little girl thought about this for a moment. "Doesn't it hurt your fingers to cut like that?"

"No," I replied sheepishly, and then tried to hide the big, red bump that had permanently blossomed on the side of my index finger from holding the scissors wrong for so many years.

"Here," she said knowingly, "I'll show you." She put the scissors in my hand the right way, and then moved my fingers up and down. The scissors inched forward, leaving perfectly cut paper in their wake. "See how easy that is?" she beamed with pride. "Now you try."

Here's the thing. I didn't want to try, because I knew I wouldn't be able to do it, or at the very least I'd look like a total goon.

"It's okay." She encouraged, sensing my reluctance.

Seeing no way out, I took a deep breath, and then slowly guided the scissors around my paper turkey. Things went fairly well for a few seconds...until I got to the first sharp turn. I lost my grip, the scissors slipped, the blades came down and instantly chewed their way through my left index finger, causing a gash that resembled a gaping red mouth to appear right there on my digit. Blood angrily spewed out of my finger's new orifice like it had been waiting its whole life for this moment to speak, and boy did it have a lot to say. As you can imagine, both my little instructor and I were surprised—not to mention queasy (at least I was).

"I think I'll go play in dress-ups," she quickly sputtered, and disappeared. I grabbed the nearest thing to stop the bleeding, which unfortunately was a Clorox wipe. Searing pain shot up my arm to the part of my brain that stores all that colorful language usually associated with sailors and rap artists. It took every ounce of strength not to let any of that verbiage fly out of my mouth. My constraint almost caused me to have a stroke.

As I danced around the classroom like a maniacal medicine man, drops of blood dripped on the butcher paper the teacher had set out on the pint-sized tables for a painting lesson later. Mortified that I had messed up her lesson plan, I tried to wipe the blood off the butcher paper, only to turn the barely noticeable red dots into big, sweeping swaths of crimson brush strokes reminiscent of a Monet painting. Honestly, it looked pretty cool, if it weren't for the fact that I was getting lightheaded and on the verge of losing consciousness.

Sensing that either A) I was about to have a seizure, or B) one of the kids had had a potty accident (that's always the first assumption when anything goes wrong in preschool), the teacher came over to find out what the heck was going on. When she saw my hand covered in red goo and my O+ artwork she asked in her most cheery, yet slightly irritated, preschool teacher voice, "Miss Stacy, did you get the finger paints out before free choice is over?"

"No," I mumbled, fighting to prevent my eyes from rolling back into my head. "I cut myself, and my hand is draining blood faster than a kosher meat shop.

She finally noticed my seeping wound. "Oh geez, that doesn't look good," she said nonchalantly like the seasoned preschool teacher she was. "Why don't you go get that taken care of while I clean up this mess?" Unfazed, she scooped up the butcher paper while simultaneously cleaning the floor with a rag under her foot. (Impressive.)

Meanwhile, the other preschool teacher (who immediately caught on and wanted to keep the kids away from the bloody mess) calmly clapped her hands and announced "Good news, children! Recess!" (Man, I swear, nothing rattles a preschool teacher.)

"But it's not time for recess," corrected a bright little boy who hated modifications to his routine.

"Yeah, after free choice we always do art," chimed in a little girl, as she headed for the bloody art table.

"Not today," said the teacher blocking her path. "Get your coats on, *please*, and get outside *now*." She gave the kids that scary teacher stare that says *I mean business* (which, by the way, still makes *me* sit up and listen).

After the doctor sewed up my finger, I called my cousin and told her what happened. "Are we even?" I asked.

"Are you kidding?" she replied. "I still have to comb my hair a certain way to cover the scar."

"But now I know how to use scissors. I can finally cut your hair without maiming you."

"Oh, really? And just where did you get this newfound knowledge?"

"At preschool. Where I also learned how to get bloodstains out of a parquet tile floor without using your hands, *and* to paint like the masters using only organic materials."

"Remarkable," she deadpanned. "I guess it's never too late to go back to school to get a *real* education."

Towels Gone Wild
(Blood and Gore, Part 2)

The other day I was at my friend's house when we suddenly had one of those little-kid mini-emergencies that didn't *quite* call for paramedic attention; however, it did require quick parental response. Apparently my friend's five-year-old had watched *Man vs. Wild* on the Discovery Channel the night before, and as a result decided to go "mountain climbing" on the laundry room shelves while his mother and I enjoyed mutual cups of coffee on a snowy morning.

What *were* we thinking?

Of course Junior fell, taking an entire shelf down with him, the contents of which gnawed up the poor kid's head pretty well. The resulting scene was gory. Anyone who walked in would've thought we were shooting a low-budget horror movie. Blood was everywhere, being that even the smallest head wound causes bleeding faster than Freddy Kruger on a caffeine bender. (See *Blood and Gore, Part 1*.) Needless to say, Junior was howling holy murder, and with every wail more blood pulsed out like a gory fountain. Yep. It was charming.

"Quick, get me a towel out of the guest bathroom!" My friend commanded with the authority of a platoon leader.

"I'm on it!" I ran down the hall into said bathroom, yanked on the cabinet door, and to my astonishment, it defiantly yanked back and slammed shut. Stunned, I tried again, but then quickly realized that the cupboard door, in fact *all* the doors and drawers in the bathroom, *had been childproofed*.

"Okay, don't panic," I said to myself, all sweaty and flustered. My kids were little once, and I, like every crazy new mother, had secured all things hinged in my house before my firstborn could even crawl, so breaking into a childproofed linen closet was no challenge for a seasoned mom like me.

Or so I thought.

I tried every trick I knew to get that stupid door open, but every time the damned thing snapped shut like the jaws on a bear trap.

"Could you hurry it up, please?" my friend screeched in that high-pitched, panicked voice moms use when they're trying to pretend they're not panicking. "I don't have enough fingers to plug all the holes in Junior's head."

"I can't get your linen closet open!" I yelled back, still tinkering with the door like it was a Chinese puzzle. "What's the secret?"

"Oh. That. Okay, first line up the two tabs to create a slot, then you put your index finger in, then you take it out, rattle the door, then you put your finger in again and shake it all around. Does that make sense?"

"Uh, yeah, if I were doing the friggin' hokey pokey! But all I want is to get one of your damned Laura Ashley towels out of the closet so we can put a tourniquet around your kid's head!"

"Oh, not the Laura Ashleys," she replied pragmatically. "Use the Martha Stewart K-Mart collection instead. My mother-in-law gave us those."

"If I can't get this open, we're going to have to settle for an oil rag out of the garage!" I grunted through clinched teeth. By this time I had one leg wrapped around the toilet for leverage and the other foot pressed against the adjacent wall, hoping to pull the door open by sheer force, which I'm here to tell you STILL did not work.

"Oh, for pity sake," my exasperated friend sighed as she dragged her bawling child down the hall to join me in the bathroom, leaving a trail of smeared blood across the hardwood floor in her wake. (Now it really did look sinister.) "Here, let me do it." She pushed me aside and with the aplomb of a safe cracker applied several secret handshake-like moves in and around the cupboard until it gleefully popped open within about five seconds.

All this for a towel.

"Good golly, even Paris Hilton's privates have more public access than whatever it is you've got locked up in that closet!" I bellowed. "What the hell have you got in there?"

"We just want to keep our kids safe," my friend replied defensively.

"From what? Criminal linens? Wash rags gone bad?" I peered in the cupboard and pulled out a bottle of expired Echinacea. "You don't even have any *real* drugs in here!"

I mean, honestly, must child locks be *that* secure? What toddler is going to use that kind of brute strength to break into a linen closet? Hey, I'm all for locking up the liquor, prescription drugs, mommy's special bedroom toys, and above all (if you must have them) guns, but just because a parenting magazine declares you should childproof your entire home after your bundle of joy takes up residency, that doesn't mean you have to put a lock on the toilet seat that only Houdini could figure out. I think a little common sense goes a long way when deciding which cubbies you truly need to board up in order to be safe.

As for my friend and her son, we finally got the bleeding to stop (with a towel) long enough to take him to the emergency room, where the boy received several stitches, of which he couldn't have been more proud if he'd won them in a knife fight. Afterward Junior recounted an exaggerated version of his exciting morning to the doctor, who then asked, "So are you going to climb anymore shelves?"

"Oh, no!" The now wiser boy replied confidently. "I'm never doing THAT again!"

And you know what? I bet he won't. Sometimes the best lessons are learned the old-fashioned way (childproof locks not withstanding). It's amazing how a life experience as small as a bump on the head can improve a child's memory when it comes to avoiding stupid stunts (well, at least until they're in high school, anyway).

Pre-stressing Over the Right School

Yesterday I overheard two moms in the grocery store talking about the schools their kids had applied to and whether or not they thought they'd get in. I have to admit, my ears grew big on this one, since I have a sophomore in high school, and I know our family is destined to walk this same path in just a few short years.

The moms in the store went on about the pains of soon having to pay thousands of dollars in annual tuition (one even thought she'd have to get a second job), but then quickly added that it was worth it because the education these prestigious schools provide would give their children the leg up they need to get ahead in life. I caught snippets of words like "academic excellence," "high test scores," "private school," "financial aid," and "French Club."

As I lingered over the fancy cheese case, pretending to read every label on every individually wrapped hunk of Limburger, I grew increasingly frustrated that the gabbing moms still hadn't mentioned the names of these coveted institutions of higher learning. Geez Louise, I thought, how rude of them to make me stand there and eavesdrop for so long, when I could be home spying on my neighbors instead.

"We're dying to know if little Pugsly got in," said one mom, obviously still too attached to her son if she's prefacing his name with diminutive adjectives. I pictured a six-foot, smelly teenager who played linebacker on the varsity football team. "We applied for early decision, so I hope that helps." I leaned on my shopping cart, causing it to discretely close in.

"We applied for early decision, too. But that won't help one bit if our Carlton doesn't get his act together and figure out *how to pee in the potty.*" The cart slid out from under me, and I hit the floor like a sack of cat litter, taking a pyramid of Gouda down with me.

"Oh, that," said the other mom, as I quickly tried to rebuild the Eiffel Tower of cheese. "Pugsly isn't potty-trained yet, either. But it's only March, and I figure we still have until September to convince him to give up his pull-ups."

OMG, they were talking about PRESCHOOL!

Since when does being in the right preschool guarantee your child will get into the Wharton School of Business when he turns 18? Honestly, I'd be a little more concerned that my kid had mastered scissors, and yet *still* preferred relieving himself after a big meal with the help of heavy-*dooty* Huggies.

What is this obsession with *the right* preschool? I thought preschool was just a way to socialize your kid and get Junior out of your hair for a few hours (two birds with one stone, if you will). Yes, we've all read about the *benefits* of preschool—how kids who go to preschool can do calculus and speak Latin by the first grade (even if they were never taught either one). But do we actually believe these urban legends? I'd sooner suppose that Walt Disney *really was* cryogenically preserved after his death than buy into the fact that my kid will be able to do the family taxes before he hits puberty—*if he goes to the right preschool*.

Oh sure, we all want our kids to have the best head start, but let's be honest. Preschool is just glorified day care that mercifully comes at the point in your parenting career where you're about to snap like a stale pretzel due to the fact that you're so tired you haven't been able to finish a thought or get out of your sweats for the last three years. You want to know the real benefits of preschool? They're quite simple, really:

- You get to brush your teeth.
- You finally have time to clip your toenails.
- You can talk on the phone without locking yourself in the bathroom (and while you're on the phone you can actually use adult language—if you can

remember how).

- You can take a shower that lasts longer than a *Bob the Builder* video.

- You can finally put some thought into getting dressed (but unfortunately, this is when you find out that none of your pre-pregnancy clothes fit).

- You can make what *you like* for lunch without some pint-sized food critic declaring, "That's icky."

- You don't have to spend the last half hour of your trip to the mall retracing your steps searching for a lost binky, blankey, mimi, pookey, num-num, cuddle-buns, or some raggedy stuffed animal so frayed and mangy it looks like roadkill scraped off the Jersey Turnpike.

- You can go to Costco and leisurely peruse every aisle and enjoy the free food samples without having to abandon your full cart in order to find a bathroom for a toddler urgently shrieking, "Potty so bad! Potty so bad!" only to come back less than 10 minutes later to find that some Good Samaritan put all your stuff back on the shelves.

Say what you want about the academic benefits of preschool (for your child), the truth is preschool benefits us (the parents) even more. It's that free-floating life raft that allows you to go to lunch in a restaurant that doesn't encourage you to color on a placemat while waiting for your cocktail to come. So as far as I was concerned, just about any preschool that kept my child safe and appropriately engaged was a winner.

But apparently I was wrong.

It seems some parents start shopping around for *the right* preschool immediately after the commencement of morning sickness. *Really?* A few preschools even require a deposit at that point! You don't think that money might be better spent on, oh, I don't know, a college savings plan instead? (Just a thought.)

When I mentioned my grocery store reconnaissance mission to my friends, many of them admitted that even *they* had stood in line overnight, back in the day, a full six months in advance of their kids starting preschool, just to make sure their kids got into the preschool of their choice. Man, I don't know if I'd go through all that even for Springsteen or Rolling Stones tickets. (Okay, maybe I'd do it for Springsteen tickets, but they'd have to be for somewhere in the first three rows, front and center.)

I fully admit that both my kids went to preschool (which now feels like a million years ago), and truth be told, by the time each one went I was ready for them to be out of the house those precious three mornings a week. And they were excited to be with new adults, preferably ones that didn't look like they wanted to go back to bed the minute they got up.

However, I did NOT stand in line overnight to get them

into preschool. In my case, ignorance was bliss. I didn't even know there *was* a process for getting into preschool, and that a person *did not* simply walk in unannounced and sign her kid up at the last minute on a whim.

Even though that's exactly what I did.

In late August, when Son #1 was three, I went to the only preschool in town I knew of and inquired if they had any openings for fall. Turns out three families had dropped out *that day* because their darling little geniuses were accepted into a gifted preschool 30 miles away, so they jumped at the opportunity to pay $8,000 per year, per kid, and left the local preschool they had so faithfully stood in line for. I immediately signed my kid up, and was even happier to find out that the preschool to which I'd just committed was a co-operative, which meant I had to help out in the classroom at least one day a month, and in exchange our tuition was kept ridiculously low. Sounds good to me.

My friends tell me I was lucky, even back then, that I got my kids into *any* preschool without preplanning, let alone such a good one. They assure me that getting your toddler into the right preschool has always been akin to getting your teen into an Ivy League college.

Oh, please.

As I mentioned earlier, we have the big college hunt coming up soon, and even though I want my kids to find schools that fit their needs, I don't plan on standing in line overnight somewhere just to get them in (unless it involves Springsteen tickets).

I'm sure when the time comes we'll be shelling out a wad of cash for college tuition, but I'm not too concerned because we squirreled away all the money we would've spent on private school (including preschool) into a college fund instead. So now the only big obstacle we face is whether or not my boys will get into the schools of their choice. But even so, I'm not too worried. I'm sure they'll do just fine, because after all, they *are* both potty-trained.

That Old-time Religion

Religion is a tricky thing when you're raising kids, because you never know if they'll be comforted or traumatized by it. By the time you figure it out, it's usually too late. (Catholic school—need I say more?) And even if you elect to send your children to church, there's no guarantee your moral and spiritual beliefs will be interpreted by your child exactly the way you see it.

Take, for example, my friend whose seven-year-old somehow got it in his head that the more you put in the collection plate, the better "seat" you'll get in Heaven. (Excuse me?) So to make sure he was guaranteed the front row at whatever Broadway-type festivities eternal life has to offer, this kid "appropriated" cash from his mom's purse to give to church, AFTER she had already given him money to put in the collection plate. In his mind, God would forgive him because the end justified the means. Now I seriously doubt his Sunday School teacher taught him that, but I can see how a seven-year-old could connect the dots to reach such a misguided conclusion.

Which is exactly why I volunteered to teach Sunday School the year my eldest turned five. For no apparent reason he suddenly decided he needed to hear the word of God straight from the horse's mouth. Being that we weren't particularly religious, I wanted to be in on the action when the Bible lessons were being doled out, even though I had about as much business teaching Sunday School as I had performing brain surgery.

When I was little my family moved a lot, so my religious upbringing consisted of going to whatever garden-variety church was handy. As a result, I attended a hodgepodge of services, including (but not limited to) those of the Baptist, Presbyterian, Lutheran, Methodist, Catholic, Unitarian, and Jewish faiths. And since my parents would just drop me off (they never went to church with me), I was at the mercy of whether or not they wanted to sleep late on Sunday mornings.

But that was okay, because religious consistency really didn't matter to me. Going to Sunday services was all well and good, but to be honest, for me church was the same as being on the yearbook staff at school or enlisting in Camp Fire Girls. It was simply another extracurricular activity that allowed me to broaden my ever-expanding social circle. For some strange reason I got grounded a lot as a kid, so I'd join any legitimate group my friends were in just so we could hang out. In eighth grade I even signed up for catechism, which ensured that I got to hobnob with my gal pals every Tuesday night at seven, no matter what my incarceration status might have been at home. It wasn't until about two months into the year that the catechism teacher realized I wasn't Catholic. The tip-off came when I defended divorce over staying in an unhappy marriage and then argued that the baby Jesus was probably black (or at least dark-skinned).

After that I was asked not to come back to catechism.

So as you can see, I was totally qualified to teach Sunday School to kindergarteners.

Eventually I found out that my toddler wasn't yearning to attend church because he had burning questions about the meaning of life. No, he wanted to go because *his* best friend went to church. (Obviously, the nut doesn't fall far from the tree.) Plus, it was common knowledge among the neighborhood small fry that this particular Sunday School served Hostess snack cakes and some nasty purple punch as the midmorning munchie, neither of which my kids ever got at home. I mean, geez, how am I supposed to compete with a house of worship that endorses Ho-Hos?

Which by the way is such an unfortunate name for a snack cake popular among kids. Especially when the little darlings forget to mention the second "Ho." You haven't lived until you've heard a three-year-old at Sunday School ask, "Can I have my *ho*, please?"

"It's Ho-Ho," I'd correct. "Like the noise Santa Claus makes." Which also opens a litany of adult comedy that didn't exist a generation ago. It's like when the theme song to *The Flintstones* ended with "We'll have a gay old time." They just didn't know what they were setting themselves up for back then.

So here I was, a middle-aged baby boomer who marched for women's rights and separation of church and state while attending college in Berkeley at the tail end of the sexual revolution, teaching Sunday School *in Utah*. And wouldn't you know it, my first lesson was...Genesis.

Now I confess, I've read *The Bible*—both Testaments. You couldn't have gone to as many churches as I had and not cracked open The Good Book once in a while. So I was quite familiar with Genesis. But even as a kid I had trouble with the whole "God created the world in six days" thing. I mean, come on, where'd He get the building materials? Particleboard and the circular saw hadn't been invented yet, and there was no Home Depot. But since I came from the *children-should-be-seen-and-not-heard* era, I kept my questions to myself. Hopefully, my Sunday School students would do the same.

And they did...at first. I opened my Genesis lesson with

the requisite "In the beginning…" and from there explained to the kids exactly what God created on each day. They listened intently, as if I was relaying the greatest story ever told (which, depending on your point of view, I was). Then when I got to the seventh day, and revealed God rested because He was tired from all that heavy lifting, they looked at me with total confusion.

"Why would God be tired?" said one little girl with such confidence I had no doubt she'd be making more money than Bill Gates by the time she was 25. "Isn't He divine? Tired seems like something only people could be. Why would He need to rest?"

"Yeah, and what about the dinosaurs?" questioned a little boy wearing a bow tie. "They started 245 million years ago and then lived for the next 180 million years."

"Where'd you hear that?" I asked.

"On *Bill Nye the Science Guy*," he replied. "You didn't say on which day God created the dinosaurs."

"I think it was the fifth day, when He created all the animals," I replied.

"But you said on the fifth day God created all the animals EXCEPT the birds and fish. And birds are direct descendents of dinosaurs," chimed in a little girl with thick glasses and an overbite.

"Okay, then it was the fourth day. And by the way, if you're going to attend church, you have to stop watching

Bill Nye the Science Guy."

"Now wait a minute," challenged the kid in the bow tie, "you said humans were created on the sixth day, and dinosaurs were created on the fourth day, but people and dinosaurs never lived on the Earth at the same time. So how is that possible?"

"Jesus, who let these kids in here?" I prayed under my breath as I stood there like a dumb bunny.

"Uh, well? Um…" For the first time in a long time I was speechless. It was obvious these kids had me by the shorthairs, so I decided to just come clean. "Okay, here's the deal. There are two schools of thought on this. One is that God created the Earth in seven days, just like I told you. And no, I don't know exactly how the dinosaurs fit in, and I'm not sure why God had to rest when He was all done. And the second thought is that the Earth's creatures have evolved from lower forms of life—like dinosaurs—and evolution continues even today. In either case, it's up to you to decide which to believe. And that's all that matters."

They suddenly got silent, and I wondered if I had traumatized them. "Any questions?" I dared to ask.

"Yeah, can we have our hos now?"

"It's Ho-Hos, and yes, you can go get your snack." They raced out completely unaware that they had brought me to my knees in one of modern society's greatest debates. Good lord, I thought, it's catechism all over again. As soon as they go home and tell their parents what I said, I'll be banished from Sunday School forever. Fired from church after my first day as a Christian missionary. How pathetic is that?

The following week I kept waiting for the inevitable "verbal spanking" I'd get by the religious police. Frankly, I was afraid to come back to church, being that I was worried the congregation would haul me to the altar, where everyone would engage in the first public stoning since the Salem witch trials. I mean, what kind of moron brings up evolution in a Genesis lesson?

But miraculously no one gave me even the slightest snub. In fact, everyone seemed happy to see me. The kids must not have spilled the beans to their parents. Or so I thought, until one mom, whom I barely knew, came up to me and said, "Chelsea loved your Sunday School lesson last week. We've been discussing it ever since."

"Um…and that's a good thing, right?"

"Absolutely! We really appreciate you giving the kids perspective." She smiled and then joined her husband in the front row. (Wow! I thought. Priority seating. They must really stuff the collection plate.)

Turns out not one parent complained about my Genesis lesson. In fact, I was asked to come back and teach kinder Sunday School after my son had moved up to the next class. But after my exhausting year of pitching Bible stories I decided to retire from the clergy. The pressure of having to hold up the religious end of a Socratic discussion with scientifically-informed kindergarteners was just too much for me to handle from week to week. When my students brought up Doppler radar and global warming during the Noah's Ark lesson, I said, "That's it. I'm out."

We don't go to church anymore because my kids' passions for high school jazz band, basketball, space camp, and a host of other extracurricular activities take up all our family time. And like God on that seventh day, we need Sunday to rest.

But still, I often reminisce about my one year as a Sunday School teacher. Ironically, going back to Sunday School as an adult gave me insight into children that I may not have received until much later in life (if ever). As a fairly new mom at the time, I figured out then that you should never underestimate kids and always engage in their discussions with an open mind (especially the ones that involve dinosaurs). No matter how young they are, or quiet they appear, children constantly form thoughts and opinions that are way more complex and wise than we think. And Lord knows we can learn from that. It took me going back to Sunday School after a 25-year hiatus to figure that out.

Sometimes God really does work in mysterious ways.

Picky Eaters

Cooking for my family is not unlike searching for the Holy Grail. In fact, I have a better chance of breeding Sasquatches to sing opera or locating a family of aliens in Area 51 than I do of finding a meal that everyone in my house will eat.

Now before I go too far down this path, I have to tell you that I deplore making special meals for picky eaters. I must also tell you that before I had kids I was the perfect parent, mainly because I had no idea what the hell I was talking about when it came to raising kids. For example, I was cocky and judgmental whenever I saw a mother wrangling a crying toddler in the grocery store or a defeated dad trying to entertain a cranky baby on a transcontinental flight. "Why can't these people control their own children?" I'd say to myself in a huff, as if I had the wisdom Mother Goose.

But after I had a couple of "young-uns" myself, my high-minded ideas about not catering to picky eaters went right out the window. In fact, most of the politically-correct parenting standards I had before kids came along seem downright silly and impractical now. As a result, I'm the first to admit I'm a hypocrite. (Which eliminates much of the stress in my life, and allows me to win lots of arguments, since I don't hold myself accountable for anything I might have said 10 years or 10 minutes ago.)

Anyway, once my little princes' chompers came in, they demanded something heartier than breast milk, which was fine by me. At the time, I was more than ready to reintroduce the occasional margarita or martini (to me, that is, not to the babies).

For Son #1 I followed protocol and offered rice cereal and mashed bananas when he was still a baby, both of which he adorably spit back into my face, and then grinned so big I thought he was going to follow up with a joke and a reminder to tip the waitress. (I don't care what any of those parenting pundits say, babies know *exactly* what they're doing way sooner than we think.) Of course, I tried other healthy foods, all of which my little boy either smashed into his hair or shoved up his nose. (Those pictures, by the way, are coming out at his wedding.)

But then somehow we stumbled upon Nutri-Grain Cereal

Bars. Don't ask me why I gave a baby a Nutri-Grain Bar (actually, I think he might have had his first one when he found it in the couch cushions at a neighbor's house). Anyway, he would eat Nutri-Grain Bars until the contents of his diaper turned purple (he liked the blueberry ones), which made me wonder if he might be ODing on Nutri-Grain Bars. So we introduced other kid-friendly foods until he gave the green light to saltine crackers, cheddar cheese, and fresh strawberries, and then suddenly ("Hal-le-lu-jah!") we had ourselves a four-course meal that Little Man would eat. Unfortunately, it was the *only* meal he'd eat, but hey, at least I didn't have to come up with creative ideas for baby's dinner every night.

I would've felt guilty about feeding Son #1 this mundane cuisine three times a day, every day until he was four, had Son #2 not come along (before Son #1 was out of diapers, I might add, but that's another story). Now I was too busy to worry about what Son #1 consumed, unless it required a stomach pumping afterward.

Compared to Son #1, figuring out what Son #2 liked to eat was akin to learning algebra while enduring a migraine—just when you thought your head hurt too much to crack the code, you'd have a breakthrough, only to find the next time you tried it, it wouldn't work. Yes, Son #2 liked carrots on Monday, but then by Wednesday he treated them like contaminated waste. But in place of carrots he'd eat French fries—until Saturday, when all of a sudden he hated French fries, right after we ordered him a plateful at Chili's.

This food merry-go-round seemed never-ending. Out of frustration, I even tried feeding him in the bathtub during his "tubby," thinking eating while splashing would make meals more fun. But all it did was make meals more soggy—and thus less desirable to baby. (Don't even get me started on the mess.)

Then I thought, well, he must just have a sophisticated palate. So I introduced "exotic" foods, like sushi, risotto, and hominy (okay, so that last one is not so glamorous, but I bought it by accident thinking it was corn and was NOT about to waste it). True to form, he'd consistently eat any unusual food I put in front of him (in fact, he'd appear to love it) UNTIL we ordered him a plateful at a restaurant, at which time he'd show his appreciation by throwing it across the room, where it'd land in someone else's cocktail, usually that of a "perfect parent" who'd didn't have kids.

I was so desperate to get healthy food into that child I even considered involving outsiders (not the professional kind, just random people on the street). Once when I saw a guy with an amputated leg in an airport, I toyed with the idea of asking him if he'd tell my toddler his leg got that way because he didn't eat the cooked vegetables his mother put in front him. But then I came to my senses when I realized such an episode might be just a little too traumatic—for the guy with the missing leg.

But for all the food failures I had with my boys, once in a while I'd achieve success. About 10 years ago I found an old recipe in my college footlocker after I'd cleaned out the basement. It was in Berkeley's school paper, *The Daily Californian* (*The Daily Cal* for short), one of those underground hippie rags that printed items you'd never find in any mainstream publication. One of which was a recipe for brownies that contained a certain ingredient that, shall we say, was a staple of the counterculture. Well, I got the bright idea to take out the secret ingredient and replace it with chopped kale or thawed frozen spinach.· And you know what? My kids loved it! That is, until one day when my younger son noticed stringy green pieces in his brownie after he'd taken a bite and promptly declared it to be grass (ironic, huh?). From then on he wouldn't eat the brownies, but for a short time I had actually snuck kale and spinach into his little growing body.

So even after all of the exhausting food wars with my kids, it was still BABIES: 100, MOMMY: 1 (I'm giving myself credit for the brownie-laced-with-spinach episode, even though it was short-lived). I had one child who would consume *only* the same things everyday, and another that wouldn't eat the same thing twice. I quickly learned what it

---

· This was long before Jessica Seinfeld wrote her kids' cookbook on how to sneak veggies into brownies. And since my version stemmed from my brush with the counterculture, and because I'm about a million times older than Jessica, I'm going to claim she stole her recipe idea from me—even though we've never met (or even spoken).

meant to be a short-order cook, which went against ALL the perfect parenting rules I stubbornly clung to before I had kids.

But once thrown into real-world parenting, I quickly learned that the academic world and reality are parallel universes. Just because a book tells you that your child may grow up to be a serial killer (or "cereal" killer, as the case may be) if he doesn't eat his peas, that doesn't mean it will happen. To me family harmony (or family "hominy" – okay, okay, I'll stop now with the "corny" jokes) is much more important than dictating what my kids will eat, so if that means I have to boil an egg for one kid, while the other one has pasta, so be it. I don't think that makes me an overly-indulgent parent (*lenient* maybe, *lazy* definitely, but certainly NOT *overly-indulgent*).

Now if you'll excuse me, I need to go make a down payment on a new Lincoln Navigator for my 15-year-old son.

P.S. My boys are now in the teenagers, and they eat so much I need a pantry the size of Rhode Island to keep up with their appetites. So much for *teaching* them to like food. Somehow they just figured it out for themselves.

Over the River and Through the Woods

A friend just told me that she and her family are going to Costa Rica for spring break. Imagine that—Costa Rica with the kids. That sounds both fun and nauseating, in the same way that riding the Tilt-a-Whirl at any minor-league amusement park makes me want to laugh and barf at the same time.

Judging by the uncertain look on my friend's face, I could tell we shared the same unspoken concern over traveling halfway around the world with a small tribe of whiners (including a husband who a freaks out if he enters an area not serviced by at least two bars on his cell phone—good luck with that).

"How old are your kids again?" I asked. Now that I'm done with elementary school, I lose track of everyone else's countdown to freedom.

"Ten, eight, seven and five," she replied with exhaustion.

"Uh-huh. And just so I don't inadvertently say something stupid, let me clarify. You are looking forward to this, right?" There's no accounting for taste when it comes to family vacations.

"Um, sure. I mean, it's Costa Rica—beaches, rain forests, exotic animals, great coffee. What's not to like?"

We both nodded and stared at each other for a few seconds, silently waiting for the other one to crack first.

"Okay, fine," she finally confessed. "I'm looking forward to being there, I'm just not looking forward to *getting there*."

And there you have it. The truth about modern-day family travel. If only we could beam ourselves to our destinations like they do on *Star Trek*, we'd all be as adventurous as Lewis and Clark. But now with less flights, more connections, TSA, full body scans, luggage searches, and not being able to bring large amounts of liquids or ointments on a plane because some crazy terrorist might pilfer it from your diaper bag and use it for God knows what ("I'm sorry, ma'am, but this 6 ounces of Desitin butt cream is classified as a felony weapon"), air travel with kids has become about as much fun as a root canal.

I speak from experience. One of my sets of parents lives in the British Virgin Islands, so of course, we've been taking our kids down there since they could barely walk. But it literally takes four plane rides and 22 hours of travel just to get there. This includes sitting around countless airport lounges watching talk-show pundits pontificate in Spanish, French, or Dutch (and sometimes English) on airport TVs with really bad reception. I'm a creative person, but there are only so many ways you can play peekaboo or I Spy with even the most patient of toddlers.

Case in point, one time my younger son (who was then six) started whining in the San Juan airport because I allowed his older brother (who had just turned 10) to help my husband hoist our carry-on bags onto a conveyer belt for one of our many TSA searches. Apparently this was a coveted task.

"You let him do everything, and I don't get to do anything!" exclaimed my younger son.

"He's older, so he gets to do stuff first," I replied logically.

"I never get to do anything!"

"You'll get to do the same things he does when you reach his age."

"Why do you give him everything he wants?"

"I don't!" I barked back loudly, quickly coming to the end of my last raw nerve.

"Yes, you do! How come he gets everything?"

That did it. Something in me snapped, and the filter (which has worn thin over the years) that usually intercepts the steady stream of smart-ass remarks that runs through my head like a ticker tape completely disappeared.

"Oh, for cryin' out loud, because we like him best, okay?" I yelled, knowing that would put an end to it.

As expected, my son made an annoyed face and grumpily put his nose in a book, very accustomed to my brand of sarcasm.

However, the older Puerto Rican lady who had been sitting next to him listening to this exchange was not (accustomed to my sarcasm, that is). She looked at me with wide, accusing eyes that seemed to say, "How could you?"

I just stoically glared back at her and said, "Well, we *do*. Like the other one best, I mean."

Then *she* got up and gruffly stormed off.

Sweet Jesus in short pants, whatever it takes. At least I finally got some short-term peace. In a world where it takes every ounce of energy I have to get my kids from A to B, sometimes the end does justify the means.

Whoever said "Half the fun is getting there" never had to take two car seats, a stroller, a box of Huggies, six puzzles, a Game Boy, crayons, coloring books, saltines, juice boxes, two tired toddlers, and a partridge in pear tree on an international flight in coach. I think all that alone allows me to say whatever the hell I want while traveling the tricky road of parenthood.

Mom Jeans

When I was a kid, it was an annual ritual to shop for new school clothes with my mom. (These were the days when you actually dressed nicely to go to school, unlike now when it's a badge of honor to have your underwear peek out over the waistband of your baggy pants.) She would haul my sisters and me to Lloyd Center in Portland, Oregon, which at the time, with 104 stores, was the largest shopping center in the world. (They didn't call them malls then, they were *shopping centers*). She would cram her three girls into dressing rooms in Lerner's, J.C. Penney, or Meier and Frank, threaten us with death if we left, then bring us hordes of clothes to try on. We didn't know it then, but we had our own personal shopper.

Fast forward to now, when all my close friends (including my two sisters) and I have collectively spawned all sons and no daughters. Not growing up with boys, I had zero experience with males and shopping, other than witnessing the few times my dad held my mom's purse so she could better assess the quality of twin set sweaters.

I don't remember what possessed me, but a few years ago I convinced two girlfriends that it'd be fun to take our collective five sons (ages two to seven at the time) holiday shopping the way my mom did with my sisters and me. It'd be a memorable day, I assured them, including lunch at a sit-down restaurant, where we'd gauge the morning's progress and then plan our afternoon like a platoon embarking on a strategic mission.

Like lemmings following their leader off a cliff, my friends eagerly agreed that a day of holiday shopping with our little boys would be a *delightful* way to spend a Saturday. (Obviously, they were new at this, too.)

Our first stop was TJ Maxx, where we piled our brood into two dressing rooms. One of us stayed with the boys, while my other friend and I went on reconnaissance. As I searched for the perfect pair of size 6x khakis on a messy display table that looked like it had been pillaged by rats, I caught a glimpse of a Winnie-the-Pooh-clad butt disappearing under a rounder of rugby shirts. When I investigated, I saw it was a child from our litter, who had escaped the dressing room and was clutching a women's purse I didn't recognize. I immediately called my friend on her cell.

"Hello?" she answered.

"Hey, could you do a head count of our kids?" After a pause, she exploded in terror when she realized she was one short.

"That's okay. I have him right here. But unfortunately, he's snatched someone's purse." Right then I heard through the phone a woman scream, "Oh my God, my purse is gone!"

"I'm on my way," I said and hung up.

As I entered the dressing rooms, the sweetest little voice cooed, "Why is your back so fat?" I turned the corner just in time to see my son and another little man from our group watching a woman check herself out in a mirror. The kids looked at me. "Mom, how come her tummy pokes out like her butt?" At this point, it was too awkward to pretend I didn't know these kids. The woman looked at me with disdain, retreated to her dressing room, and slammed the door.

Right then my other friend returned with armloads of clothes. "Who's first?" she asked cheerfully. Suddenly another dressing room door opened, and a woman appeared holding a two-year-old at arm's length like he was toxic waste. "Is this yours?" she said, irritated. "He's been crawling between dressing rooms."

Now Purse Woman appeared from nowhere, grabbed her satchel from me, and unleashed unhelpful and unwanted advice on how to raise kids. (Another childless perfect parent, no doubt.)

"I trust this will all make sense later," my friend who'd just returned whispered to me.

As we took our lumps from Purse Woman, the whole episode came to an abrupt halt with the sound of breaking glass. We all ran out to the floor area, and standing next to a shattered display amidst what looked like broken Faberge Eggs stood my friend's son and another kid I didn't recognize. My friend's son looked at us wide-eyed, pointed to the kid next to him, and calmly said, "He did it."

"Time to go," I quickly muttered.

Which brings me to my lesson learned that day. Just because my sisters and I had a great experience doing something as kids doesn't mean our kids will enjoy it, too. We were different children defined by a different time. And as much as I want to share my childhood with my boys, some things are best left as stories told by the fire on a winter evening.

The other thing I learned is that shopping for clothes with boys (as with men) is an oxymoron—like *military intelligence* or *nonworking mom*. Even though there are words to describe it, it simply does not exist in the real world.

So instead of civilized afternoons of shopping followed by lunch in tearooms where the waiters wear white gloves, my sons' shopping memories will consist of gathering around the computer and selecting clothes online from Overstock.com and the Lands' End website. Or going to a garage sale and finding several pairs of Levis an older kid quickly outgrew. And you know what? They're just fine with that. If their pants end up being a bit too big, they can always wear a belt.

But unfortunately, when it comes to shopping for *my* pants, *my* rear end is not that forgiving. Buying women's jeans online is like committing to a mail-order husband. The chances of him working out are slim to none, and you certainly don't want him hanging around after you realize that no matter how hard you try to make him work he will never compliment your ass.

After giving birth to two 9-lb. babies (not at the same time, thank goodness), I can't just simply buy a pair of pants off the Internet and expect them to make me look like anything better than a broomstick with a big butt (if broomsticks had butts, that is). Therefore, I still have to purchase my wardrobe in real stores. However, I'm now smart enough to know that I absolutely SHOULD NOT let anyone who possesses a Y chromosome tag along.

So the other day I went shopping (alone) for jeans, which if you're over 35 is just as humbling as trying on bathing suits during those bloated times of the month when you want to rip off someone's head just because they looked at you funny when you asked them to take out the trash. (Or is that just me?) There's something about gazing into a three-way mirror at your keester packed into denim like a big, blue sausage that makes you want to hurl. I think it comes from getting lightheaded when you realize that no matter how much you exercise and avoid gluten you eventually end up with your mother's ass.

Part of the problem is the fashion industry's unexplained embrace of super low-rise pants. Granted, it's been a while since I've shopped for jeans (sweats have served me well, thank you very much), so I need to know, at what point exactly did clothing manufacturers decide it's flattering to make jeans end just above your pubic bone, causing every ounce of midriff fat you own to cascade over your beltline like a heaving lava flow? Honestly, does my butt crack *really* need to debut itself to the world if I bend more than 30° at the waist? I can't even get a box of Special K from the bottom shelf at the grocery store without the risk of ending up on the Internet as a *before* picture in some e-How article. ("How to Tame Your Butt Cleavage and Still Look Sexy Over 40." Oh please, are you kidding me?)

Now I admit, I think I'm a fairly fit woman for my two score and ten years on the planet (yeah, that's right, go figure it out), so imagine my surprise when the sales girl at Nordstrom's brought me several pairs of jeans that not only had purposeful rips in strategic places, but also had waists that you couldn't even squeeze a volleyball into.

"My name is Lavender," the barely 20-year-old whispered to me as if she were revealing where all the weapons of mass destruction were hidden. "If you need anything, or have a question, just let me know."

"Actually, Lavender, I do have a question," I whispered back, equally serious. "Do all these dressing rooms come with complimentary liposuction? Because unless the one I'm in has it's own fat-sucking spigot, there is little chance I'll be able to squeeze even one butt cheek into these *fabulous* jeans, which by the way, could double as a hand puppet."

"They'll be fine," she reassured me.

"I don't see how…"

"Just try them on."

"But there isn't enough material to…"

"They stretch to three times their size."

Oh, now that hurt, because even though they needed to be bigger, they didn't have to fit a beer keg.

"They're a Spandex blend," she continued, using that exasperated tone I reserve for my son when he puts an empty peanut butter jar back in the cupboard. "A size 6 can fit up to a size 10."

"But then…it really isn't a size 6, is it?"

"It is until you put it on." And with that, Lavender shut the door and left, leaving me alone with a pile of pants that were just slightly larger than Barbie clothes.

Determined to prove my point, I grabbed a pair of jeans and shimmied into them. True to her word, they did stretch far enough for me to get them on. However, they clung to my skin like a rash and stopped six inches below my naval. My bottom half was packed in so tight I had butt cleavage all the way up to my shoulder blades. I didn't even have to bend over in order for my backside to crack a smile at anyone who happened to be unfortunate enough to be standing behind me. (I'm sorry, but I don't care how good of shape you're in, a public display of middle-aged butt crack is just icky. For years we made fun of plumbers for it, and now it's a fashion statement for women? I don't think so.)

And to make matters worse, this particular pair of jeans had a bunch of rips in them that I swear collectively spelled out the words "help me" across the seat, as if my fanny was in need of assistance because I tried to suffocate it in a hermetically sealed pair of bell-bottoms. (And by the way, when did *those* come back?)

Suddenly, there was a knock on the door. "Everything okay in there?" It was Lavender. She'd come to gloat, no doubt. "Can I get you anything?"

"Yes, I'd like my pre-pregnancy hips back, please."

"Excuse me?"

"Nothing, I'm good."

She swung open the door, and it was all I could do not to mace her.

"Oh my god, those jeans look absolutely *magniriffic* on you," she squealed in her best *I'll-say-anything-to-make-a-sale* voice.

"If by "magniriffic" you mean I look like a denim zit

about ready to pop, then I would have to agree."

"Let me bring you the next size up."

"The eights that are really twelves?" I asked with mock enthusiasm.

"Exactly! I'll be right back!"

I frantically spent the next five minutes trying to peel those suckers off, doing a series of gymnastic moves and yoga poses that I was in no shape to perform. Apparently, Spandex likes to go on, but it hates to come off. Maybe that's how they get you to buy the jeans—once they're on your body, they have to be surgically removed, so you have no choice but to pay for them.

Eventually, I did get the jeans off (miraculously, without the jaws-of-life or any other outside assistance). And upon doing so, I snuck out of the dressing room before Lavender had a chance to come back and insist that camel toe is the hot, new look this year for the AARP set. (Ewww.)

I quickly left the mall and headed for Target. Once inside, I made a beeline to the women's department and bought what can only be described as *mom jeans*, which are comfortable on so many levels, mainly because there's no risk of them sliding down to my thighs if I bend over to get groceries out of the car. The thing is, they actually look good on me. I know this because my best friends have told me so, and they wouldn't lie (not to my face, anyway, which is all that really matters).

But I'm okay with wearing mom jeans because, after all, *I am* a mom (I have the stretch marks to prove it). So if that means I can't encase my rear end in the latest designer jeans because I don't have the body of a 25-year-old anymore, so be it. I've got something better: the ability to walk into a room wearing mom jeans and not give a rat's ass what other people think. Because I know in my heart that no matter what goofy outfit I might happen to be wearing that day, I can leave the house confidently knowing that I look absolutely, 100% *magniriffic*.

The Superhero at Home

One day, back when my kids were in elementary school, I showed up to my son's fifth-grade classroom to bring him the sack lunch he'd forgotten that morning on the kitchen counter. Yes, I know I should've just made him eat the school lunch (a fate worse than death, as far as he was concerned), but I figured bringing him his lunch gave me a reason to come snoop around the school without the responsibility of volunteering and actually being expected to do something productive while I was there.

As I walked down the fifth-grade hall I noticed on the walls hand-made posters of pretend newspapers called *The Me News*. The posters were supposed to be the front page of a mythical daily paper that told all about the kid who created it, for example, the child's birthday, favorite sport, and what he or she wants to be when he or she grows up. They were also apparently asked to list a hero and the reasons they found that person heroic. Most kids noted people who are larger than life, like Shaun White (because he won lots of Olympic medals), Albert Einstein (because he was smart), and Justin Timberlake (because he can sing and dance). And some even went so far as to idolize the likes of Spiderman, Magneto, and Wonder Woman. But one kid seemed to put a little more thought into picking his champion. Instead of wracking his brain for some extraordinary being, he simply wrote, "My hero is my mom, because she listens to me and makes me feel safe."

This caught me off guard. I know this kid, and even though he's a good person who seems to have his head on straight, I wouldn't have pegged him as someone philosophical enough to see the value of good parenting at age 10. I mean, come on! Can there really be such a child?

I decided to find out for myself, starting in my own home. That night, after our bedtime reading ritual, I told my second-grade son that we were going to play a new game called "That's What I Like About You," where we each say one thing we like about the other.

I went first. "I like your sense of humor," I said. "You can make almost anything funny. So if I'm sad, chances are good that you can cheer me up." He was very pleased with this assessment, and I think surprised that I was so honest. "Okay, your turn," I prodded.

He pondered for a moment, playing with the frayed edge of his blue security blanket, then looked me in the eye and said, "I like that you make me do the right thing." Now it was my turn to be mute for the better part of a minute. I couldn't speak because the sting in my eyes was contributing to the lump in my throat. It was all I could do to not fall off the bed.

If you take the time to listen, sometimes a kid's honesty hits you square in the heart. On the surface my son's statement appears to be all about him and what he likes, but the subtext tells a deeper story: *I know I'm not perfect, but I count on you to make me better*. I can't think of a bigger leap of faith that anyone takes for anything else.

In the following weeks we played more rounds of "That's What I Like About You," and I have to admit that every evaluation my son had of me was not some perfect pearl of wisdom. Most of the time he said things like "I like that brown coat you sometimes wear," or "I like that Grammy is your mom," or "I like that you let me watch TV more than my friends." (That one I wasn't so proud of.) But every once in a while a glimmer of insight innocently peeked out, the most rewarding one being, "I like that you say what you think is right." Now, for anyone who doesn't know me, that statement taken out of context could mean a lot of different things. But to fill in the blanks, I am politically active in local government and our school district, so he has seen me lobby for educational causes, as well as go before City Council to plead for something as simple as a sidewalk. So what he's saying is *I like that you stand up for what you believe in.* I like that about me, too, but I never would've guessed he noticed that trait, let alone admired it. I can only hope that he admires it enough to one day emulate it.

So returning to my question, can there really be a child who "gets it," in terms of what we're trying to accomplish as parents? I think the answer is *yes.* In fact, if you ask your child what he thinks of you (and you *really listen* to his answer), you might even find such a kid in your own home.

As for the superhero mom I read about at school, I ran into her at the grocery store later that day. "Did you know that your son thinks you're a hero?" I asked.

She just laughed at me. "I seriously doubt that," she replied. "Last week I had to ground him and his brother for using my Epilady razor to shave the dog. I don't know what the heck we're going to do with a bald Malamute." She hurried off before I had a chance to tell her that her son's edition of *The Me News* was dated yesterday.

Camp Humble

I, like every mom and dad I know, got into parenting for one reason—the money. No, wait. That's why I got into the stock market, which in retrospect was about as smart as skinny-dipping in a kiddie pool full of hungry gators. Now why did I get into parenting again? Oh yeah, for the rewards. Not the monetary kind, mind you, but the kind you get when you actually do something with your kids. And when I say "do something," I don't mean stick them in front of Wii Sports while you savor margaritas on the back deck with the other moms in the neighborhood (although now that I mention it, that sounds like a really good idea).

No, what I mean is to actually *go somewhere* and *do something* that both adults and the small fry will enjoy. A Disney cruise comes to mind, but since most of us have already maxed our second and third home-equity lines of credit for things like braces, health insurance, and food, you might want to start smaller. Disneyland itself is always an option, but unless all the kids in your family are over 48 inches tall, either Mom or Dad will have to sit out Space Mountain with a crying short person, while everyone else in the family repeatedly rides the dang thing until they all have herniated necks. Besides Disneyland isn't cheap. A family of four might as well look into what it costs to go rock collecting on the Galapagos Islands instead.

Since we live at 7,000 feet, with snow on the ground six months out of the year, by President's Day we're all so ready to be someplace where the temperature peaks above 50 degrees that we'd even consider going to Boca Raton during a Medicare convention. And to make matters worse, our school district closes the entire week of President's Day, so my kids see no reason why they should have to sit around the house just waiting for their turn to shovel the driveway while their rich friends head off to Rio de Janeiro to attend jai alai camp.

I always try to convince my kids to wait so we can travel the week of Independence Day, because by then we don't have to go to another time zone to be outside and warm at the same time. (And can I take a moment to say that *Independence Day* as a holiday is such a misnomer? Yeah, yeah, I know it's called Independence Day because that's the day our country became independent from Great Britain; but let's face it, there's nothing *independent* about a trip where you have to pack for everyone and be the keeper of a roll of on-the-road toilet paper, hand sanitizer, and AA batteries—this is why my purse is the size of a small rock formation.)

Regardless, since the economy is still about as dependable as a wet diaper, we can't afford to shoot the wad on a vacation in February, which immediately eliminates Hawaii, the Caribbean, or Boondocks Fun Center in Draper, Utah. So I got to thinking…how about we go (drum roll, please) camping!

Stay with me here. Yes, I realize that February in the Wasatch Mountains still constitutes the dead of winter, but I figure if you drive south long enough, you'll eventually find some sun. (And for those of you who live in Southern California, Arizona, South Texas, or anywhere along the Gulf Coast, well you just have no excuse for not getting out on President's Day weekend. You and your year-round flip-flops. You're the only people I know of in the continental United States who can use the words *Tommy Bahama* and *Martin Luther King Day* in the same sentence. Bah humbug!)

Camping is not only an inexpensive way to force everyone in your household to interact and "have a good time, damn it, whether you like or not" (which is the mantra of any middle-class family vacation), it's also a great source of entertainment for the kids when they get to watch Dad (the pencil pusher) pitch a tent and try to start a fire with two sticks that aren't matches. Even if Dad was an Eagle Scout, remember that was a long time ago. The knowledge behind merit badges earned in 1982 has an expiration date of about 2002 (and that's stretching it), whether Dad wants to admit it or not.

Mom's also a laugh a minute on a camping trip. Kids, if you really want to see that vein pop out on her forehead, don't forget to ask her why her rear end looks so big in her Banana Republic hiking shorts, and by the way, what are all those purple and blue lines all over her legs? After Mom engages in a delicate discussion of the word "varicose" with a fourth-grader, there's always the joy of cooking over an open fire, only to hear "You promised us In-N-Out Burger on this trip."

So where's the joy in camping with your kids? Okay, here it is. Nothing endears you more to your children than looking like a buffoon in front them. These little people think you are the most amazing thing next to God. Every day you miraculously solve all their problems, ranging from Math Olympiad to "Why is my brother such an idiot?" In their inexperienced eyes, you are infallible. That can be pretty intimidating, and as we've all read in our millions of parenting handbooks, intimidation does not equal respect. Letting your child watch you fail, and then laughing about it, makes you even more extraordinary to them (which by definition should make me downright remarkable to my kids by now). There's nothing wrong with your child seeing you struggle outside your element, because honestly, we all struggle every day (but thankfully the kids are at school so they don't get to witness it). And what better gift can you give your child than to show him the world doesn't end if your marshmallow falls off your stick into the campfire?

So yes, camping is a cheap way to get your family together (even in the dead of winter) and at the same time reveal your human side to your kids. And if you're a great camper, well, then you're just going to have to find some other way to look like a goober in front of your children. Fortunately, there are always bowling and skateboard parks as back-ups.

A Tale of Two Generations

When I became a parent late in life I was smart enough to know that I had no idea what I was doing. This revelation came to me in two parts, the first being the monumental moment my husband changed a diaper for the first time when our son was only hours old. Even though the disposable diaper sagged off our skinny little boy's torso like a mumu on a ballet dancer, we both evaluated my husband's handiwork and thought it was good. That is, until the pediatrician came in and said, "Uh, yeah, it's on backwards. The animals on the waistband always go in the front." Oh. There's a *front* on a diaper?

The second "aha moment" that made me realize we might be in over our heads was when a nice nurse at the hospital wrapped my firstborn in a cotton blanket, handed him to me, and then booted us out the front door with a hardy handshake followed by, "See you next time the stick turns blue."

"That's it?" I said. "You're just going to let us take this child home? Where's the user guide?"

"You'll figure it out," she said, checking to make sure we had secured the car seat properly, and that like the diaper, we hadn't put him in the darn thing backwards.

Now I have to admit, I am the oldest of three girls, and both my sisters are quite a bit younger, so when my first baby came along I did have *some* parenting skills that had I learned by helping my mom. However, I was a child of the '60s, and the whole concept of raising kids back then was a little different.

For starters, we had cloth diapers (with no backs or fronts), diaper pins (I'd like to take this moment to formally apologize to my youngest sister for accidentally sticking those pins in her torso more than once), glass bottles, no breast pumps, no microwaves, no Diaper Genies, no baby videos or music, and other than *Howdy Doody, Leave it to Beaver*, and *Captain Kangaroo*, no children's TV (this was even pre-*Sesame Street*). Nothing was disposable. We washed and reused *it all*. Everything was sterilized by boiling it in a pot on the stove, and diapers were dried by hanging them in the basement in the winter or on a clothesline out back in the summer.

When I was four I happily stood up on the bench seat of

my great-grandmother's '54 Chevy sedan *while she drove,* and I didn't even know what a seat belt was until my parents bought their first new car in 1964 (a Plymouth Valiant, by the way, with push-button transmission—the car I eventually learned to drive on and drove all through high school).

I mention this bit of nostalgia to show that my *Wonder Years* mid-twentieth century upbringing was of little use when I started my own family in 1995. Things had changed dramatically by then, and in between my leaving home and having my first child, I didn't bother to evolve when it came to childrearing. Why would I? I was too busy learning the Electric Slide.

But I'm here to tell you that patience really is a virtue, because if you wait long enough everything old *really does* become new again. As shown by my middle-school son, who discovered the nuances of The Beatles, as a result of *Beatles Rock Band* hitting the streets. All of a sudden, he's telling me that Paul is the walrus, and that when George Harrison croons about his guitar gently weeping it's a veiled reference to the singer's troubled relationship with his ex-wife due to the fact that she married Harrison's best friend, Eric Clapton. (Say what, little man?) He loves the idea of "An Octopus's Garden" under the sea, but yet can't understand why anyone would want to be "Back in the U.S.S.R." when there is no such place. (This did open the door to a history lesson.)

Similarly, last year this same child entered a school

talent show as a juggler and wanted to use The Allman Brothers' instrumental "Jessica" as his performance music.

"Great!" I said. "Did you select that tune because it's a classic all the parents will love?"

"No. I picked it because I wanted to use a *Guitar Hero* song." And then he added, "What do you mean by *classic*? *Guitar Hero 2* has only been out since 2006."

Again, another history lesson, this time on '70s rock.

I have to admit, I'm diggin' my younger son's interest in the music I loved as a teenager. He plays it loud, like I did, only this time the big sound blares out of a tiny iPod docking station, whereas I played my albums on a huge console stereo that took up an entire wall in my parents' dining room. I can still hear my mom screaming above The Who's "Baba O'Reilly," "Turn that crap down!"

There are other small nuances creeping into my children's lives that remind me of my own childhood. For example, our local dairy switched to glass milk bottles, which we have delivered to our house. Our elementary school converted to "homemade" hot lunches (cooked from scratch by real lunch ladies), as opposed to simply microwaving processed food. Record players and vinyl are making a comeback, as are first-generation video games, like *Pong*, *Pac Man*, *Galaga*, and *Centipede*. And much to my mother's chagrin, my son wants to wear his hair long, like John Lennon during his Yoko Ono period (I told him at best he gets to wear a Jim Morrison—yet another classic rock lesson).

So as my kids get older, I'm finding a lot of what I learned when I was young is returning to the teenage collective consciousness. Somewhere along the way my childhood experiences became as relevant to my parenting as finding an old skate key that had been lost for years. It's lucky I'd had it all along, because suddenly "skating" is cool again. Who knew I'd someday be so hip in the eyes of a longhaired, mini-hippie, Beatles-loving, twenty-first century tween?

Confessions of a Band Geek Mom

Whoever said kids get easier as they get older must have been talking about their pet hamster. Not since the rebuilding of civilization after the fall of the Roman Empire has life been busier than it is right now as my husband and I try to accommodate my tween and teen sons' crazy schedules.

This is not to say we let our kids sign up for every boneheaded activity that comes along. However, we also don't let them sit at home watching *South Park* until their eyes dry up like little raisins (a fact which, I'm told by my younger son, makes me an unfit mother).

Since our kids are interested in lots of things, they have tried IT ALL over the years: soccer, baseball, basketball, tennis, swimming, art lessons, piano, acting, track and field, cooking, science camp, and bowling. And since we live in a mountain resort town with retired Olympic venues, they got to participate in activities most kids in other parts of the country only dream of: ski clinics, ice skating, bobsled, luge, mountain biking, and horseback riding. I even signed them up for cotillion. But truthfully, that was my idea, and as such I had to drag them to those dinner dances, making deals along the way that usually involved large sums of cash and an unlimited laser tag punch card. However, I must say that now when they occasionally give me their nasty teen and preteen hormonal sass, they do so with courtesy and finesse.

"Mom, may I please go Patrick's house?"

"Will his mom or dad be home?"

"I don't know."

"Then, no."

"Um, Mom, I don't mean to be rude or disrespectful, but you're acting like an overprotective dork."

"Uh-huh. Duly noted."

Anyway, as they got older and schoolwork got harder, they were forced to limit their extracurricular activities. And being that my husband and I are cheapskates who really don't want to pay for every whim our kids get talked into by their friends, we made them each choose one activity and let the rest go.

So they picked music.

Brilliant, we thought! We win! No more sitting on cold, snowy fields watching our skinny kids get pummeled by gargantuan opposing players (good-bye, soccer). No more wasting entire Saturdays at boring double-headers waiting for our kid to come up to bat, only to watch him strike out (good-bye, baseball). No more icing injured limbs because refs won't call fouls on aggressive players (good-bye, basketball). Yes, music would be easy because all we'd have to do is show up at the occasional recital, which last I checked was never held outside in the dead of winter, and it didn't require special gear that you could only order from a pro shop in Norway (shipping not included).

As we smugly gloated about our good fortune to the parents of the Junior Olympic Ski Team (who have to tote their offspring all over the Rockies) it soon became apparent we didn't know what the hell we were talking about.

See, here's where it all took a weird turn; our kids actually *practice their instruments*. This definitely falls into the "be careful what you wish for" category, because when they practice diligently not only do you have to listen to the same scales, arias, and arpeggios over and over until you want to stick a knife in your ear, but they also get better.

And when they get better, everyone from pep band to the all-state honor band to high school varsity jazz band to wind ensemble to marching band to the school play pit orchestra wants them on their team. And naturally, they have to take private lessons for each instrument they play, so say their band instructors. (Uh, excuse me, but what is it exactly that *you're* teaching them during band?)

Between our two boys you can always hear at least one (sometimes two) of the following musical instruments being played at our house: piano, flute, clarinet, alto sax, tenor sax, soprano sax, baritone sax, oboe, bass clarinet, bassoon, and drums. This is what happens when they practice—they get handed more instruments. Literally. We don't even buy them, and yet somehow the strangest noisemakers mysteriously show up in our house! (Although in the long run, we usually end up coughing up the cash to purchase or rent our own versions. Once the kids get even remotely proficient on the darn things they insist on upgrading. It's kind of like letting your kids get hooked on crack, except that with musical instruments there is a possibility they can use their talent to pay for college without getting arrested.)

I'm telling you, when people hear that your kids practice instructors, neighbors, friends, friends of friends, and even long-lost relatives (and friends of long-lost relatives) come out of the woodwork bearing unused musical instruments they are more than happy to get out of *their* houses. "Call it a permanent loan," they say. (I'm still not exactly sure where the oboe came from. One day I heard this funky noise, like a duck being slaughtered, coming from my son's room, and I ran in to find this scrawny reed instrument glued to my kid's lips. At first I thought maybe our bassoon and flute got together and created a love child. But then I heard a rumor that the band teacher at the high school lent him an oboe so he could practice at home over the summer. *Do they really do that?* I thought. Hand over an exotic instrument like that to just anyone? Yeah, they do. If it's an oboe. P.S. Earplugs not included.)

And then there are the concerts, recitals, band tours, and competitions, not to mention the cost of instrument repairs, band uniforms, sheet music, airline tickets (for the band tours), and of course now I'm going to varsity football games, even though I hate football, just so I can watch my nerdy little band geek boys play Queen's *We are the Champions* on the saxophone and flute every time some Neanderthal scores a touchdown.

Suddenly I'm clocking in more mileage on my Subaru Outback than a bus driver on tour with the Grateful Dead and forking out more cash than a busted ATM machine.

Whine, whine, whine...well then, if it's so darn inconvenient, expensive, time-consuming, and sometimes even heartbreaking (for example, when your kid doesn't perform well even after he's practiced a piece more hours than he sleeps in a week) then why do my husband and I do it?

We do it because every time one of my sons performs a solo that people applaud wildly for I see a little more confidence in his face. We do it because now my kids FINALLY understand what it means to be on a successful team, even though they aren't competitive. We do it because art and music are the first to go in school district budget cuts, and that breaks our hearts. We do it because music teachers are overworked and underpaid, yet they'll give up entire weeks of their summer (without pay) to put together a marching band for a small-town Fourth of July parade. We do it because it keeps our kids busy and out of trouble. We do it because it may pay for their college someday. But most of all, we do it because it's their passion, and I can't think of anything more rewarding than watching my kid do something he loves (even if sometimes it sounds like a sick cow—I'm talking about you, bassoon).

So if you'll excuse me, I have to go pick up my son from orchestra pit practice. His high school is doing *Kiss Me Kate* and he's playing second-chair reed instruments. Look for me on opening night. I'll be the one in the front row marveling at how great the band makes the actors look.

Carpool Number 32 on Driveway 6, You're Cleared for Takeoff

I'm a little worried about my family's carbon footprint. I think it's a men's size 14 and growing. For four people who live in a town so small you could literally walk across it in less than an hour, we drive way too much. Ironically, we're not motoring around just so we can go to the store and back. No, we get into our cars and leave our fair city at least twice a week to go to (are you ready for this) *band practice*.

Yes, my sons joined a state honor band, which at the time seemed like a good idea, until we realized that the band director lives about 50 miles from us. Hmm…call me psychic, but I'm guessing this guy is going to want the kids to travel to his end of the GPS map for practice. (It would be too much to hope it'd be the other way around.) When I suggested to my older son that he literally phone in his performance, he just looked at me as if I had the common sense of a fence post (being he's a teenager, I'm getting used to that look).

So here we are at one of those parenting crossroads where you ask yourself, "Just how far should I go (in our case, literally) for my kids?" Before you have children you almost always answer that question with "as far as it takes." But once you have them you realize there's a fine line between support and indulgence, and you're never exactly sure where that line falls, or if you should even attempt to cross it.

For us, we decided to support our sons' decision to be in the state honor band, however we knew we couldn't do it alone. I'm a firm believer in the concept of "misery loves company," so we talked other young, talented, local musicians into joining the state honor band and then lo and behold we had ourselves a carpool. Yes, I admit my encouragement of these kids was partly for selfish reasons, but hey, it's not like I was pushing them to join a cult or something. … Okay, so maybe it is a little like joining a cult, but at least the uniforms are way more fun (if you don't count how much they cost).

Luckily one of the moms in our carpool was proactive about organizing a driving schedule. Kudos to her, because had it been up to me we'd still be slugging through Mapquest just trying to figure out where the heck the rehearsal space was, which at the time changed weekly due to commercial space issues. Turns out a 25-person big band makes A LOT of noise. And after just one rehearsal in each new spot the neighboring tenants would say, "Uh, yeah, I don't think so. Buh-bye." (I'm happy to say the band has since found a permanent home.)

So Proactive Mom e-mailed out a calendar and asked all the parents to sign up for the times they'd like to drive. When no one responded, she went ahead and scheduled the families. Well, of course this got great response and it went something like this:

Parent 1: "Oh dear, I'm afraid we can't drive on the 12th because Derrick has an orthodontist appointment. Can we trade with Sully on the 5th?"

Parent 2: "That's fine, as long as Sully can drop out of next month's schedule. He has soccer play-offs until the 27th."

Parent 1: "Okay, so for our first trip I can drive, IF the kids take a bus to the dog park and wait for me to pick them up in the parking lot."

Parent 3: "Will the bus driver let them on with their instruments?"

Parent 4: "What if I drive the instruments down earlier in the day, then someone else can bring the kids later. I can take everything except John's upright bass."

Parent 3: "I'll bring that. I have to make an airport run anyway."

Parent 1: "Then why don't you just take all the instruments down and back in the first place?"

Parent 3: "Because I'm picking up out-of-town friends, and between the extra bodies and all the ski equipment they bring I won't have room for anything else."

Parent 1: "Oh shoot, you know what? I just realized that even though I can take the kids, I can't stick around to bring them home."

Parent 2: "I can drive down and get them."

Parent 3: "Okay, so who's doing what now? I'm lost."

Parent 1: "I'm driving the kids to band practice."

Parent 4: "I'm driving their instruments to practice, except for John's bass."

Parent 3: "I'm driving John's bass."

Parent 2: "I'm picking the kids up after practice."

Parent 1: "So we have four parents in one carpool, and we're all driving to the same place on the same day?"

Parent 2: "Uh, yeah, I guess so."

We all look at each other in confused silence.

Parent 1: "Okay, works for me."

Parent 2: "Me, too."

Parent 3: "Yeah, I'm good."

Parent 4: "Ditto."

I think we just increased our carbon footprint to size 15 DDD.

Some Days It's Good to Be a MANIAC

Now that my boys are getting older and (sort of) independent I have more time to myself, which means I can do things like go to the grocery store without having to use the shopping cart with the bulky kiddie car attached to the front. (I swear it's like trying to navigate a Winnebago on Maui's Road to Hana to get that thing around a display of spaghetti sauce without it ending up a free-flowing red river of marinara meandering down aisle three.) It also means that when I'm out I can pay attention to what's going on around me, because now I'm not constantly looking for a child who has either gone missing or is (hopefully not) the cause of a big scary crash in Williams Sonoma. (Don't even ask me what I was doing in a Williams Sonoma with little kids.)

This distance has given me the opportunity to watch other

moms with their kids and realize that, like Pop-Tarts, we moms come in many different flavors. Truthfully, however, I've known this since the early days of my eldest son's preschool experience. The big tip-off was when I happened to be in the classroom when a mom brought in a homemade birthday cake for her four-year-old son that put the mini reproduction of Mt. Rushmore at Legoland to shame. The cake was an exact replica of a Bionicle (a Lego robot, for those of you without boys), and it actually made beeping noises and lit up when you pressed its claw. She also had matching plates, napkins, hats, and goodie bags (my introduction to this annoying tradition) that included an age- and gender-appropriate brainteaser puzzle for each child. (Thanks a bunch. I couldn't solve it, so now I look like a dunce in front of my kid.)

Just so you know, on my son's birthday I brought in Fig Newtons, but forgot the juice.

Even though this mom is a dear friend of mine and she will always have a special place in my heart, I have to say with all the sisterly love on the planet and the deepest respect SHE IS A RAVING LUNATIC—better known by therapists as a Type A Mom, or as I just heard recently on *The Today Show*, the "Wife and Mom-in-Chief." But because I like things categorized in ways that make sense to me, I'll simply refer to moms of this ilk as Mothers Against Negligence In All Circumstances, or MANIACs for short.

A MANIAC is a woman who has unlimited crafty talent and seems to run on an endless battery. She's the room mom who puts the rest of us to shame because, like MacGyver, she can fashion an entire third-grade classroom holiday party out of a box of paper clips, a toilet plunger, and a bolt of red seersucker she just happened to have in the trunk of her car. Her kid is the one at the school Halloween parade in the Cruella de Vil costume that looks like it came straight from the Disney backlot, only to find out she whipped it up the night before while waiting for her homemade organic chocolates to harden so she could individually wrap them for the neighborhood kids (and by the way, she made an extra batch for the needy—in India).

On the other end of the spectrum is what psychologists refer to as the Type B mom. This mom means well, but somehow drops the ball more often than not, usually because she's trying to juggle parenting with some other crazy folly— like earning a wage. You can always spot a Type B mom roaming the halls at school. She's the one wearing flip-flops even though it's November and there's three feet of snow on the ground. That's because she still hasn't found time to dig out her one pair of winter footwear that she stuck in the attic last spring to make room for the six million pairs of tennis shoes that litter the house come May.

In my case, however, the letter "B" doesn't even begin to accurately describe the cavernous gap between the Type A moms and me. For my category you need to skip all the way down to the end of the alphabet. I'm not afraid to admit that I'm a Type Z Mom, or what I like to call the Zero Effort Domestic, conveniently referred to as the ZED Mom for short. And as I've come up through the public school ranks, I'm relieved to find out that I'm not the only ZED.

The ZED mom is happy to take her turn volunteering in the classroom or carpool, however, it's not unusual for her to occasionally space out on these duties, in which case thank goodness the MANIACs are there to pick up the slack. ZEDs are also known for dropping their kids off at school while still in their pajamas (the moms, not the kids—okay, sometimes the kids), showing up late—or completely missing—back-to-school night (honestly, who reads all that junk that comes home on the first day?), and sending their precious little ones off to school with a sack lunch of two-day old cold pizza and a Red Bull.

Now just like there are many shades between blue and yellow on the color wheel, there are many types of moms between MANIACs and ZEDs. These are the hybrid moms who don't reside on either end of the spectrum, but hang out somewhere in between, like…

POLITICO MOM

This fiery mama is the gal who gets involved in every political cause from "Should we serve more than two starches in a school lunch?" to "Is the cookie dough fundraiser really a plot by the Communist Party?"

Politico Mom goes to every school board meeting, every city council meeting, and every planning commission meeting, sometimes while her kids are calling her from home to tell her that the smoke detector won't go off even though the fire is completely out or to ask, "Just exactly how do you apply a tourniquet again, Mom? Because little brother Joey sliced open another finger when he was trying to debone a chicken."

Politico Mom not only joins the PTA/PTO, the NAACP, the ACLU, the DNC or RNC, the NEA, MoveOn.org, and the United Way, but also runs for school site council and threatens to run for school board once her youngest hits high school. School administrators generally cringe at Politico Mom—that is until she aligns with their interests. Then they lobby her like she was Speaker of the House.

Politico Moms are easy to find in that they seek you out, usually when organizing a rally against school uniforms or picketing for a new math curriculum. They need bodies to further their causes. Over 50% of the MANIACs can be talked into crossing over to become Politico Moms, however moderate MANIACs avoid Politico Moms like a classroom full of flu-infested first-graders, and thank the Lord above caller ID was invented before their kids started kindergarten.

But ironically, as obsessive as Politico Moms are about

causes, they tend to drop the ball in other, more detailed aspects of childrearing—such as making sure there's enough food in the house, and that the family doesn't exist solely on spaghetti sauce out of a jar, Lunchables, and dinosaur-shaped frozen chicken nuggets. To cover *those* delicate bases we have…

ORGANIC MOM

She's the one who'll tell you that her two-year-old is a vegan when she drops him off at your house for a play date. Really? Did he tell you that when he came out of the womb? Her kid is always the one who begs for the Rice Krispie Treats and Keebler Fudge Sticks he happened to sniff out when he was rummaging through your pantry while the rest of the kids were outside eating dirt.

Organic Mom also insists on using cloth diapers, so if you're babysitting Organic Kid you have to endure those messy drawers (even after you peel them off Organic Kid's behind) until Organic Mom can whisk them away to the dirty-diaper recycling center. In return, you get a lecture when you drop your kid off at her house with a backpack full of Huggies.

And plan on taking your child to Ben and Jerry's after you pick up your little darling from Organic Kid's birthday party, because let's face it, who is going to eat the oatmeal "fiber-licious" birthday cake or endive almond butter wraps when everyone at the party was expecting a grocery-store-bakery birthday cake (complete with the lard-based frosting), flanked by a Pokémon piñata full of Gummy Worms and Ring Pops?

But in spite of Organic Mom's penchant for everything natural, she's usually pretty realistic about Junior's mental capacity, and thus lets his development progress at its own pace. Sometimes waiting too long, for example, to give up little things like breastfeeding, in which case Junior ends up washing down his carrot cake with "mommy juice" at his five-year-old birthday party while his kindergarten friends look on in horror. (Ewww. Awkward!)

Even though Organic Mom doesn't want anything but cotton touching Junior's poor, diaper rash-plagued rear end, she also won't insist he be reading *Catch-22* to the homeless by age two. That's a task left to an intellectually obsessive-compulsive breed of parent I like to call...

INDIGO MOM

The Indigo Mom is the complement to the Indigo Child, which is a kid who displays unusual attributes in psychological behavior and intelligence, sometimes known as a *gifted* child (at least according to the kid's parents). Now I admit, truly gifted children do exist, but honestly, you have a better chance of winning the lottery in Utah (because you drove to Boise to buy your ticket) than you do of sprouting a real-live gifted child from your intellectually average loins.

The Indigo Mom, however, thinks her child is unquestionably gifted and talented (G and T to those in the know) just because the little tyke figured out how to use scissors before anyone else in preschool, even though using the toilet remained a mystery until second grade. As her offspring gets older she brags about their family dinner conversations in French, as well as her child's amazing ability to conquer Chopin preludes by first grade. And mercy me, aren't all kids reading Kafka by age 10?

Indigo Mom also thinks that everything her little miracle does is a work of art. So don't be alarmed if you walk into Indigo Mom's kitchen to find dried pesto sauce and mud painted on all the lower kitchen cabinets. It was just "little Sebastian" exercising his inner Van Gogh on a day he felt particularly inspired.

This all becomes somewhat of a short circuit for Indigo Mom, however, when in high school her kid refuses to continue with orchestra in favor of going to the skateboard park. Or worse yet, is caught smoking in the school bathroom when he's supposed to be at a National Honor Society meeting debating the importance of ethics. And if Indigo Mom gets *the call* from the police that all parents of teenagers dread, her automatic response is something like, "Why no officer, it can't be my Leland. He's down at the soup kitchen serving *vichyssoise* to the homeless."

Yes, if Indigo Mom came with her own theme music, it would be: *"The cheese stands alone, the cheese stands alone. Hi-ho the derry-oh, the cheese stands alone."*

AN AROMATIC BOUQUET

Even though it's mildly amusing to poke fun at ourselves as parents (which means we have to appreciate all the little ironies that pop up during parenthood or we'd go nuts), there are very few of us (if any) who are all one type of parent all the time. We are all virtually a sweet-smelling bouquet of neuroses. Some days we're Indigos, some days Politicos and on our lucky days ZEDs, but regardless, we should NEVER beat ourselves up about it. Because it's our kids (not us) that dictate what kind of support person we have to be that day. It's completely out of our control and that's just a fact of life.

But I have to admit there are times when the stress of not knowing what kind of mom I'll have to be when I get up in the morning makes my head spin. In those cases, after the kids are finally out of my house and safely ensconced in school, I just curl up in my ZED cocoon, turn on the Oprah channel (OWN, for those of you in the know), and dine on the stash of Girl Scout Thin Mint cookies I've been hiding in the freezer since March. That is, until one of my sons calls from a snowy street corner and gives me grief for forgetting to pick him up. (I don't know what he's griping about. They both should be used to that by now.)

Excuse Me, I Volunteered for What?

At the beginning of every school year we have back-to-school night. And at every back-to-school night those cagey people on the PTO (formerly known as the PTA—why they had to change "Association" to "Organization" at our elementary school is beyond me) post volunteer sign-up sheets for all the odd jobs that need to be done throughout the year, but that no one wants to pay for because if the truth be told, a monkey could do them. Stuff like selling refreshments at the school carnival. Raking the sand pit on track and field day. Sorting books for the book fair. Negotiating with those crazy Sally Foster wrapping paper ladies who come to your school to convince you that if your kids sell wrapping paper it will end world poverty and solve the school budget crisis. Okay, so that last one actually requires a parent volunteer with a brain, but regardless, the list goes on.

When you think about it, the PTO/PTA's strategic volunteer recruitment plan not only makes perfect sense, it's brilliant. By late August all parents are high on the idea of their kids going back to school after months of listening to the little angels complain about how unfair life is because *all* their friends got to take summer trips to exotic places like Easter Island, the Bahamas, and Dubai, while your sad brood had to stay home and mow lawns. "We didn't even go to Lagoon[*] this year," is a common whine among entitled kids whose parents suddenly lost all their disposable income in the 2008 stock market crash. As if not being able to blow chunks on The Cliffhanger or losing consciousness from the G-force on Colossus: The Fire Dragon were grounds for Child Protective Services to come in and investigate.

Suffice it to say, you'll agree to anything at back-to-school night, as long as the school commits to keeping your kids six hours a day, five days a week. ("Need a kidney for a fundraiser? Absolutely. Just promise me you won't send little Damien home before three.")

However, signing up in September to be a late-in-the-school-year volunteer (or worse, a committee chair) at back-to-school night is kind of like getting pregnant in late summer

---

[*] Utah's version of Disneyland, except in this case all the thousands of dollars we local parents spend (in one day) on outrageous admission, overpriced food, and games no one can ever win stays in Utah's economy...at least that's how I justify going to Lagoon when I should be using that time and money to clean the garage and pay off debt.

and then facing the consequences come early spring. It may have felt good at the time, but once the labor pains kick in you're basically looking for someone to kill. Just like gestation, your spring volunteer due date seems like an eternity away in that first trimester of school. However, when that weak moment occurs you can't help but give in. That's when you have that scary little talk with yourself that goes something like this: "You know, it feels *so good* to volunteer, especially since I don't have to show up until six months from now. That's so far away. Most likely it'll never happen."

Oh, but it does happen. And shortly after the new year rolls in, you get THE PHONE CALL. Usually it comes from a room mother, or a PTO/PTA officer, or a committee chairperson who is probably also kicking herself once she realizes that she, too, volunteered last fall to head up the school talent show immediately on the heels of an extended yuletide visit from her annoying brother and his equally high-maintenance family, which includes his judgmental wife and their demanding kids with their dust-mites allergies and intolerances to wheat gluten and dairy.

There is no denying that being held accountable for a casual decision you made months ago feels faintly reminiscent of getting the big baby news from your doctor. If you weren't planning on it (even though you *willingly* did the deed that sealed the commitment), it can put you into a momentary tailspin. At first you're in shock, and then you're in denial.

Something like this:

"Hello, Stacy, this is Cody Pendant. I'm the PTO president, and I'm calling because the book fair kicks off in two weeks and I see you signed up to chair this event."

At this point, I get a ringing in my ears, my mouth gets dry, and little beads of sweat pop out on my upper lip. "Oh, no, no, no, that's impossible," I mumble weakly. "I was so careful at back-to-school night this time. I didn't touch anything, I didn't sign anything…"

"I'm sorry, Stacy, but the tests came back positive," says Cody Pendant sympathetically. "Our handwriting experts have confirmed that *it is* your signature on the volunteer sign-up sheet."

And then I think to myself, "That just can't be! I wasn't even drinking at back-to-school night. That came later at home when I had to help my son with fractions and that stupid lattice multiplication method, which makes about as much sense as dividing by zero. (Damn you, *Everyday Math*! But that's another story.)"

"Hello? Stacy? Are you still there?" asks Cody. I always seem to forget that these people aren't privy to the variety show continuously running in my head.

"I'm sorry," I mutter, "but I won't be able to lead the book fair this year. I'm, uh, scheduled for, uh…, gall bladder surgery! Yeah, that's it. I've been putting it off, but my New

Year's resolution is to finally get that darn gall bladder removed."

"I thought you had your gall bladder removed last Halloween. Just exactly how many gall bladders do you have, Stacy?"

"Did I say gall bladder? I meant appendectomy. I needed to have…that, you know, thing…taken in."

"You mean taken out?"

"Yes, out. In, out, you know, it's like a revolving door down there."

She listens suspiciously, and then goes in for the kill.

"Oh, that's such a shame. Because the book fair is our biggest annual fundraiser, so if you don't do it, then the entire fourth and fifth grades will have to go without science textbooks and earthworm farms. But that's okay. I suppose the teachers could go *yet another year* explaining how microorganisms work through the use of shadow puppets."

Fine, so what am I supposed to say to that? Of course, I'll head up the book fair, or the fall festival, or field day, or the teacher appreciation luncheon, or the district track meet. Or whatever. They have me by the heartstrings and they know it.

Speaking of which, I just looked at the clock and noticed I'm late for a site council meeting at my son's middle school. Yes, somehow I got suckered into being on that board, too. Normally, I wouldn't care about punctuality, except last time I was late they elected me secretary, which means now I have to take minutes. Can you imagine? Not only do I have to show up to every meeting, I actually have to listen to what's going on! Just when I had finally perfected the fine art of looking engaged even though I was mentally composing a grocery list.

If volunteering has taught me anything, it's to always be prompt, and NEVER leave any school-related meeting to go to the bathroom. ALWAYS use the restroom before you get there, unless it means you'll be late, in which case just hold it. Otherwise, you run the risk of some MANIAC convincing the site council that fifth-grade science should be taught on the space shuttle, and if we all got our pilot's licenses (with the rocket ship endorsement) then we could take turns carpooling our kids up there.

Holy jet packs, Batman[*], it may be too late! I have to run.

---

[*] I'm dating myself here.

The Care and Feeding of Dust Bunnies

I'm the first to admit my kids are pigs. No matter how much I "remind" (i.e. nag) them to pick up after themselves, their rooms still look like crime scenes. Sometimes I can't even see the floor, at which point their junk often spreads to other parts of the house like some uncontrollable virus. Forget this silly H1N1 business, the true definition of swine flu is when my kids' higgledy-piggledy ways start taking over our home, causing a disorderly pandemic.

Even though I wish they were neater, I have to admit I totally understand their messy ways, being that I'm not the tidiest person in the world either. But regardless of my habits, I just can't bear to turn them loose into the world NOT knowing how to clean a bathroom or do their own laundry (at the very least). They're both good students and organized about other aspects of their lives, so there's no reason they can't figure out how to pick up dirty underwear off the floor and put it into a hamper located LESS THAN two feet away. Or in my younger son's case, if he can pile his dirty clothes on top of the hamper, why can't he just lift the lid and put them in it? ("It takes too much time away from other things, Mom." Really? Like what? Defeating the evil empire in *Star Wars Battlefront*?)

So in my effort to get them to appreciate cleanliness while living in a world of *my* clutter, I've employed countless motivators to encourage them to clean up their acts: taking away privileges; grounding them; screaming until my veins pop out and spell the words "crazy woman" across my forehead; bargaining with them like the guy selling watches in Times Square; giving them an allowance IF they keep their rooms clean; fining them if they don't. Nothing seemed to work. For some reason they love lounging in their own squalor (maybe because they see how much I enjoy lounging in mine).

I've even gone in and cleaned their rooms myself, bagging up (what I think are) useless items and then hiding them. My plan was when they asked, "Where's my stuff?" I'd dramatically unveil it all and if they wanted it they'd have to buy it back (or work to get it back). Trouble is, they never missed anything I hauled out of their rooms! And the really painful part was I'd end up storing all their junk until the next garage sale, at which time they'd see it in the driveway, fall in love with it all over again, and then sneak it back into the house. How is it that I could be so smart and still end up on the wrong end of that deal?

I used to think my kids were untidy because they're boys, because when I was their age I was very neat. Mainly because I knew my mom WOULD throw my stuff away if she found it lying around. (With her it was never a threat.) But I have since had parents of girls tell me that young females can be just as messy. In some cases, even more so when you count all the Barbie accessories and American Girl doll clothes (excuse me, *outfits*) piled on every surface. Or when they get older, the eye shadow left on the floor that gets ground into the carpet. Or the textured tights that perpetually hang on the shower rod in the bathroom.

Okay, so it wasn't a gender thing. That was *some* consolation.

But just when I was about to raise the white flag in surrender, we had a turning point, or rather a breaking point. My husband finally broke down and admitted that he couldn't stand our kids' messes any longer (after 20-plus years he was barely used to mine), so he started picking up after our boys. This made me completely lose it, because not only did that mean those boys were getting away with being pigs but it also taught them that eventually *someone else* would clean up their messes (or fix their problems). And since I married later in life, I'd dated enough incompetent guys to know that I didn't want to turn two great kids I love into men I couldn't stand to be around.

At first I told my husband to stop cleaning up after them. But being who he is, he couldn't help himself. "I can't bear to look at it anymore," he said so pathetically that my heart went out to him.

So I decided to go back to the source. I calmly told my boys that whenever Dad picks up their things I'll punish them, not Dad. This FINALLY got a reaction.

"But it's Dad who's doing it, not us!"

"Yeah, that's not fair!"

Oh, suddenly it comes down to *fairness*. And to them it's not fair to be held accountable for someone else's actions, regardless of what the punishment is. Interesting. I smelled blood, so I went in for the kill.

"I'll tell you once to pick up your stuff, and after that if it looks like Dad's even thinking about doing it for you then whatever you have planned for the weekend will be cancelled faster than a *Family Guy* marathon on the Christian channel. It'll be a YouTube Saturday night for you both, regardless of whose mess it is."

Of course they thought this was incredibly unjust and griped about it to no end. But I have to say it worked. From their point of view, it was one thing to be punished for what *they did*, but to have to take the hit for what *Dad did*? Well, that was just too much for them to handle. So now when they sense my husband getting annoyed with all the clutter, they immediately jump up and make sure they don't have anything lying around. And if they catch Dad picking up their stuff, they quickly take it away from him.

That doesn't mean their bedrooms have become spotless sanctuaries of clean living. I mean, after all my expectations aren't *that high*. Their rooms still look like the opening scene of a *CSI: Miami* episode. But at least now the mess is confined to their own domains, which is okay because I just shut the door and pretend I don't know what's on the other side.

As you can imagine, the irony of this lesson is not lost on my kids. They're quick to point out that I seem to tolerate *my own* messes just fine, even though *their* messes cause my voice to go up about three octaves, which puts it on par with that of a hysterical chicken. The first time they brought this paradox to my attention I smiled and carefully explained the concept of a double standard, and how I, as a parent, have earned the right to adhere to one.

This of course led to more protests (I just love how they think being a kid is so unjust), so I tried to help them make sense of it by assuring them that my mother had also insisted that I pick up after myself when I was a kid. As a result, I eventually became one with the vacuum cleaner, which led to me being a very neat and orderly adult.

Before kids, if I had a free moment I'd change the shelf paper in the pantry, alphabetize my spices, or reorganize my underwear drawer, because back then I had the time to do it. Now it's a miracle if I can even find clean underwear, mainly because it's been two weeks since I've done laundry, and that's probably because we ran out of detergent somewhere around the summer solstice and I keep forgetting to add it to my grocery list.

But since these messy kids have come into our lives I've realized that if I insist on clinging to a serious cleaning regime I will:

A)   Have no time for anything else, because I end up spending my days cleaning or fixing something,

OR

B)   Go nuts because my kids constantly mess up or break things that I need to clean or fix.

So as I continued to harp at my kids about why you have to change your bed sheets more than once a year or preached about the importance of proper aim ("How many times do I have to tell you, the pee goes *in* the toilet?"), I actually found myself caring increasingly less about *my own* general household clutter (by the way, don't tell my mom) even though I still couldn't stand theirs.

So when the kids grouse about the fact that my bedroom isn't always as clean as theirs, I calmly point out they're lucky I'm gradually mellowing or we'd all be neurotic (or at least more neurotic than we already are now). Then (sensing a teaching moment) I philosophically explain to them that as I've aged (like fine cheese) I've earned the right to bask in the delicate aroma of my own stench, if I so choose. However, I simply refuse to put up with theirs. End of story. (Ah, there's that sweet, parental double standard again.)

It's not that I've given up on cleanliness, believe me. I draw the line at utter filth (sort of). It's just that I've made friends with the fact that having a family means living with clutter—as well as dust, dirt, mud, smooshed food where you'd least expect it, Legos shoved down a drain, clogged toilets, non sequitur storage (by the way, who put the CD in the toaster?), broken knickknacks from Pottery Barn, and various human and pet stains that are too gross to describe.

When I first got married I kept a house that would turn Martha Stewart chartreuse with envy. The beds were always made. My bathrooms were always clean. And my kitchen was so spotless you could perform surgery on the countertops (just in case I ever had to do an emergency tonsillectomy on one of my dinner guests—hey, you never know).

At the time, I thought I was a hard-wired neat freak, but the fact is I simply *learned* to appreciate the beauty of a properly folded towel from my mother, who, as I eluded to earlier, is the queen of anal housekeeping. It took having my first child to understand that, like hair and eye color, a person's messy factor is part of his or her DNA. In other words, you come out of the womb either caring about heel dents on your white plush pile carpet or not.

It was such a relief for me to eventually realize that I am firmly in the camp of not caring. However, I did not go lightly into my sloppy liberation. At first I thought there had to be something wrong with me if I didn't follow my toddler around with a Dustbuster sucking up the stream of crumbs and other particulate matter he left in his wake. I mean, come on, what kind of loser was I if I couldn't keep my house clean just because there was a kid around? Never mind that I was so tired I was nodding off in the middle of the day like some old crone who'd just had her pudding.

By the time baby went down for *his* nap I was always at a crossroads. Do I:

A) Sleep?

B) Write (and earn some money)?

C) Clean up the lunch mess?

Sleeping or writing always won out. And you know what? When I woke up (or put down the keyboard) I didn't even see the lunch mess anymore—at least not until 5:00, when I had to clean up the lunch mess to make room for the dinner mess.

As time went on I increasingly ignored housework, and as a result I became a much happier person. It was as if a mop equaled stress, and somehow I had found a way to let go of both. Who knew I was such an innate slouch? If my husband even looked at me funny about any impending mess (because he did not so readily embrace my newfound Zen attitude about a muddled household), I'd just hand him the vacuum cleaner and say, "You know what to do with it, Skippy." (Which was weird because his name is George.) Suddenly cleaning the toilet paled in comparison to writing in my journal or hanging out with my kids (which gave me something to write about in my journal). I remember we'd go to the park a lot when my kids were little, because honestly, who wants to sit around a house that's in such disarray?

I completed my journey over to the dark side when my second son was six months old. My sister (who had no children at the time) and I were having a lovely conversation when all of a sudden my little Prince Charming projectile-vomited up the contents of his stomach, which included rice cereal, a saltine cracker, and the $8.99-per-pound organic blueberries that hadn't been in his body for more than five minutes. The barf shot across the room like a bottle rocket and splattered on the back of a custom-upholstered chair, where it then dribbled down the leg and made a nice purple puddle on the white carpet. It was spectacular—kind of like a Jackson Pollack painting.

Stunned by the acrobatic properties of my baby's bile, my sister and I stopped mid-sentence to witness this extravaganza, then turned our attention to my son, who was grinning from his highchair with purple goo oozing between his budding teeth. He was obviously quite pleased with himself. Nonplussed, I immediately picked up my conversation where I'd left off before I was so rudely interrupted by puke.

My sister graciously listened to me babble on, but then after a couple of minutes she couldn't take it anymore. "Aren't you going to clean that up?" she asked with so much confusion you'd think we were doing Sudoku puzzles in Lebanese.

"Clean what up?" I replied.

She made a disgusted noise that sounded like a train letting off steam, grabbed a kitchen towel, and started in on the baby puree.

"Oh. That. Yeah, I was getting to it. By the way, since you're down there, you don't happen to see a couple of dust bunnies roaming around under the couch, do you?"

"Yep. You want me to get rid of those, too?"

"No. Leave them. I've adopted them as pets."

She looked at me like I didn't have a brain cell left in my head. "Parenthood has made you weird," she touted, as she went off in search of another towel. Good luck with that, I thought. They're all dirty.

Beware of Summer Camps

Dear Mom and Dad,

   Camp Moneybucks is very fun this year. I'm so glad you bit the bullet and paid the extra $900 so I could do the adventure hikes, which included bungee jumping off Teddy Roosevelt's nose on Mount Rushmore and water skiing down the Snake River rapids on footwear we made out of redwoods we cut down in our logging class. (By the way, I don't care what any lawyer says, that thing with the buzz saw was not my fault. But don't worry, the doctor said I should regain up to 75% use of my finger once the bone has fused and the stitches come out. For now we may want to rethink that piano recital in July.)

   This has been the best summer vacation ever. I've met a lot of interesting friends here at camp. My favorite is a kid named Elmer. He's an awesome athlete, and all the kids pick him first for their teams—probably because he's so big for his age. I think this has something to do with the fact that he repeated the fourth grade three times.

The camp counselors here are very nice, too. But since they all have goofy names like Funky Pickle Lips and Booger Boy, you'd think they'd be funnier people. One night we decided to play a trick on a horticulture counselor name Tammy Swinette, and she got so upset she left camp for good crying. I mean, come on, what's the big deal about seeing your underwear run up a flagpole? The fact that she was still *wearing* her underwear when we did it made it even more hilarious. Some people just don't know how to have fun.

Yesterday we had a real live Cherokee guest speaker named Walks With Jackals come and tell use about Native American history. He even brought some old jewelry that his ancestors made. He told us it was very fragile, but obviously he didn't know what he was talking about because when he wasn't looking we tied the beaded necklaces together to make a rope swing that held together just fine. But then when Walks With Jackals saw what we did, he panicked and grabbed the swing, which was a big mistake. It broke and little beads rolled everywhere, mostly into the lake. Walks With Jackals got really mad and yelled at Mr. Swanson, the camp administrator. Can you believe anyone would get so freaked out over a bunch of old junk?

My favorite thing to do at camp is crafts class. Last week we learned how to macramé a fishing net. A kid from Crusty Creek, Idaho, named Lamont showed us how you can also use the net to create a bear trap, but since there weren't any bears around we thought it'd be funny to set the trap right outside the camp administration building. Mr. Swanson's leg will be fine once the cast comes off, but it doesn't matter anyway, because he can't get up until his neck heals. Then he can have his back surgery and start to learn to walk again. So it's all good.

Thanks for sending me to such a great place. Even though I didn't originally want to be here, I have to say this camp taught me things I never would have known how to do had I not come. I can't wait to try out some of this stuff at home. See you in a few days.

Your loving son,

Runs with Hunting Knives (That's the name the camp counselors gave to me. It was either that or Addicted to Fire.)

P.S. Did you know a regular fish tank holds the same amount of liquid as a Coke machine, including the fish? Who knew?

P.S.S. I bet that Disney Cruise I wanted to go on (but you said *no* because it was too expensive) sounds pretty good right about now…wouldn't you agree?

The Rhetorical Mom Question

When is a question not a question? I'm not even going to wait for an answer, I'll just tell you. When any frustrated mom asks her sloppiest kid, "How many times have I told you to clean your room?" Or when she asks her most defiant child, "Do you want to be grounded?" Or when she inquires of the son who NEVER listens, "Do you like hearing me nag?" Or even back in the day when I'd mouth off to my own mother and she'd reply with, "Do you want me to slap your face?"

I mean honestly, who in their right mind is ever going to answer these questions with any kind of sincerity? Everyone knows you should just take the hint, zip your lip, and move on. However, if a kid has even the slightest sense of humor these rhetorical mom questions are invitations to a verbal smackdown, a witty game of chicken, if you will. Which totally defeats the purpose, because I'm the first to tell you, if I ask one of my sons a rhetorical mom question, I DO NOT want a literal answer. I do, however, expect him to promptly get off his rear end and fix the problem that caused me to pose the ridiculous question in the first place.

For example, if I ask, "How many times do I have to tell you to pick your underwear up off the bathroom floor?" I don't want to hear some number as a response. Instead I want to see the culprit put down the TV remote, get up out of the recliner, and toddle off into the bathroom to pick up those soiled drawers that have littered the tile off and on since the onset of Y2K. No discussion, please. No debate, no justifications as to why dirty underwear is right at home on the floor. Once I make my subtle request (in other words, ask the rhetorical mom question) you know what to do, so just get up off your keester and do it. Is that too much to ask?

Now the flip side of that coin is that sometimes the rhetorical mom question is so…well, *rhetorical* that it simply begs for a smart-ass answer. And if you have a bright teenager who appreciates the politically-incorrect, subtle humor of, say, any sitcom on the Fox channel, then you have to watch what comes out of your own mouth. For example, I was in the grocery store and heard a mom ask her teenage son, "Will you watch my purse?" To which he replied, "Why? Is it gonna dance?"

Mom was not amused. (Although, I have to admit, I

thought it was a pretty snappy answer. But then again, it wasn't directed at me, and he wasn't my son.)

True, purse watching was a reasonable request on Mom's part (and let's face it, it was a rhetorical question, since she never expected her dear, sweet child to say no). However, in this case Mom made the mistake of asking her son to keep an eye on her bag, *as if he had a choice*.

Now I know parents like giving their kids choices, because it makes children feel like they have some control over their own lives. And I applaud parents who let their kids weigh in on some family decisions. However, in the interest of avoiding being the butt of your teenager's jokes (which you are anyway just by existing) I suggest you give your teen choices that constitute win-win situations for you, and, at the same time, still get your points across.

For example, the mom in the grocery store could have replaced her polite request with the more direct, "Son, watch my purse or else I'm going to give you a big, wet, sloppy kiss right here in front of God and everybody." I guarantee he will hold that purse without hesitation. Oh, he may try to call your bluff at first by offering a rebellious, "You wouldn't dare!" in which case you simply pucker up and head for his face. He'll grab your purse so fast people will wonder if they're witnessing a mugging.

So the next time you find yourself in a teenage debate over a rhetorical mom question that went bad, just stop and say to your beloved child, "I think you misunderstood, so let me rephrase." And then reword the question giving your dear, sweet offspring two choices, both of which directly benefit you. If your child appears confused, just tell him to go consult with Dad. He ought to be used to this drill by now.

Husbands in Training

As the mother of sons, I feel it's my duty to make sure my boys grow up knowing how to do at least three specific, yet important, household chores: wash clothes, clean the bathroom, and cook a meal/clean the kitchen (which I count as one job). And they have to be able to do all that without complaining or damaging anything (which is the tricky part). I picked these three mindless tasks because they're the ones I hate to do most, closely followed by grocery shopping, making dinner, and dragging those damned garbage cans to and from the street in the middle of a snowstorm (which, by the way, seems to be a moot point when the automatic arm on the trash truck almost always misses the target and consequently spews trash all over the neighborhood. Yes, by golly, I'm so glad I take the time to sort our recyclables.)

Anyway, when I got married my dear husband couldn't even brown garlic bread in a toaster oven without setting the kitchen on fire, so I'm making it my business to ensure my boys have some basic domestic skills that the future women in their lives will appreciate.

We started with cooking. Son #1 took a cooking class the summer between sixth and seventh grades and learned how to make tacos. So one day after his class he insisted on making a Mexican fiesta dinner for us (i.e. tacos). Sounds good to me. Any meal I don't have to cook is delicious as far as I'm concerned. Armed with the recipe he received in class, we shopped together for the ingredients.

After we got home, he cut up the lettuce and tomato, shredded the cheese, and chopped the onion. I gave him the pan in which to fry the ground beef and helped him hunt for all the spices he needed in that black hole we call a pantry.

As I watched him sauté onions with the finesse of a seasoned chef, I thought *just maybe* cooking might be added to the ever-growing list of things he does well. Once he tossed the ground beef into the pan, he blithely said, "I've got it covered, Mom. Go sit out back with Dad." Since it was a nice summer evening, I thought that was a splendid idea.

Sitting in our backyard, taking in our view of the Waterfall ski run at Park City Mountain Resort while sipping a Cadillac Margarita from my commemorative Hussong's Cantina mini-pitcher, I thought life doesn't get any better than this. (Unless of course, the cooking class my son took *also* taught him how to make Cadillac Margaritas, but I guess that's just too much to ask for, living in Utah.)

And that's when I suddenly heard cries of "Help, Mom! Help!" coming from the kitchen. I rushed in to find my dear son staring at the oven mitt on his hand, which happened to be engulfed in flames. I grabbed his hand and immediately drenched it under the faucet. "Why did you just stand there?" I asked with a screechy voice that sounded like a condor trying to sing rap.

"Uh, I don't know," was the most intelligent response he could muster up.

Okay, so maybe we weren't ready for cooking yet. I made a mental note to put food preparation on the back burner, so to speak.

Fast forward to present day, when I decide it's time my boys learned to clean their own bathroom. Fortunately, we have enough bathrooms in our house so that my two boys share a bathroom exclusively. This is both good and bad. It's good because I don't have to endure the cesspool their bathroom becomes in a matter of seconds after it's been cleaned. And it's bad because since I never go in there, the germy mess simply festers until a new ecosystem evolves, producing never-before-seen life forms that are so abundant I feel like they should pay rent.

But if I'm going to show my boys how to clean their

own bathroom, then I need to step into that vast unknown. So in I go. Oh, and by the way, I should add I hadn't been in there in weeks.

Suffice it to say, my boys are well on their way to bachelorhood, because no woman is ever going to put up with such *manly* bathroom behavior. The first thing I notice is that the ceramic tile around the toilet is the color of a manila envelope. This is all well and good, except that the tile was white when we put it in.

"Oh my God, is that pee on the floor?" I screech. (There's that rapping condor again.)

"Uh, I don't know. Maybe."

"You've got to be kidding me! It's a hole as big as a basketball! How can you miss when you're barely a foot away?"

"Sometimes I'm tired," my younger son rationalizes.

"So you're telling me lack of sleep constitutes bad aim? Maybe you need to go to bed earlier."

"No! I'm the only kid in the sixth grade who has to go to bed at 8:00 as it is!"

"This is unacceptable." I finalize. "You scored 14 points at your last basketball game, I know you're a better shooter than this." I turn to my firstborn. "And you! You are so meticulous about practicing your sax until you've got every note perfect. What happened to that accuracy here?"

"It's not me, it's HIM!" Son #1 counters, pointing to his

brother.

Son #2 shrugs, "Geez Mom, it's not like hitting the toilet is going to get us into college."

"I REPEAT, I did not make that mess!" Son #1 interjects. "I'm very precise." And then with all the drama of a Tom Clancy spy novel he points to his little brother and exclaims, "I'm telling you it was him! He did it!"

"Okay, ENOUGH! Strap on these rubber gloves, boys. You're going in." And with that I made them get on their hands and knees and scrub in and around the toilet until it passed my inspection. Then I showed them how to clean the sink, counter, mirror and tub. They gagged their way through it as if I had forced them to sift through a compost pile. Once in a while one of them would come out claiming they couldn't take it anymore, to which I'd reply, "Well, now you know how I felt every time I had to change a poopy diaper. Now get back in there and clean until you can eat off those floors!" (Eew, gross. That analogy went a little too far.)

Today I'm happy to say my sons clean their own bathroom on a regular basis, and since they do the scrubbing they're a little more careful about creating messes in the first place. Son #2 also sets and clears the table every night, and Son #1 cleans the kitchen. After dinner my husband and I simply leave the table and go for a walk. When we return it's like elves magically came in while we were gone and made the kitchen spotless.

We haven't gotten around to learning how to do laundry, and I haven't reintroduced cooking, but I figure we still have time. Besides, I think I'll wait until I'm ready to remodel the kitchen before we attempt cooking again. That way, in the event of a disaster I can always rely on homeowners' insurance to finance the project.

High Finance At Home

Every year in April I file an income tax extension and then complain about how the final tax-filing deadline sneaks up on me in October. It's not that I mind paying taxes. I mean, somebody's got to foot the bill for all that annoying road construction they do every summer on I-15 during peak travel times. It's just that I hate all the paperwork that goes along with paying taxes. I can barely remember how to write a check (what with online banking and all), let alone how to fill out some arcane form that makes me guess what I can and can't deduct (*no* on dry cleaning, *yes* on dry rot—what the heck?).

Good old Form 4868 is the federal government's way of enabling us procrastinators so we can put off dealing with taxes AND not land in the pokey for tax evasion. Unless of course you procrastinate so long that you eventually forget to file and pay your taxes all together. Then you're just stupid.

There are people who go for years without filing a tax return until one day you find them on TV crying "Foul!" when the IRS slaps them with a hefty bill. Every time I see this drama play out in public I always wonder, "Did this person really think he could elude taxes *simply by ignoring them*?" (Because if that were the case, I would've figured out that loophole a long time ago.)

I posed the question to a friend one day, as I stood in line at the grocery store glancing at the tabloid covers of magazines no one buys anymore because you can read *TMZ* on the Web for free. Turns out a certain popular celebrity owed millions of dollars in back taxes and he had no idea how he was going to pay his bill. "How could you get so behind on your tax bill?" I wondered aloud. "Don't you think somewhere around $200,000 you'd get concerned? Who the heck taught this guy how to manage money?"

My friend shrugged. "Probably his parents," she shot back judgmentally. This stopped me cold. For years now analysts have been trying to figure out who to blame for our country's many financial meltdowns, and now you're telling me *all along it was the parents' fault*? Do we really get all our money smarts from our parents?

I thought back to my own adolescence (which took a while because it was so long ago). I don't remember sitting through even an hour's worth of class time on how to balance a checkbook in high school. True, personal finance is not part of most states' public school core curriculum. However, now that I think about it, it should be. Oh sure, you can take finance classes as electives, but let's face it, if you're interested in signing up for *Advanced Quickbooks* as a teenager, then you're probably already light-years ahead of your peers when it comes to managing money.

This got me to thinking about my own kids, one of whom spends money faster than a horde of Mormon moms at a Big Lots! on payday. In the last few years both my kids have done odd jobs around the neighborhood, raking in cash to the tune of at least $700 EACH (and that's just during the summer). As you can imagine, their tidy little incomes have come in handy, because now *I* can borrow money from *them*. In fact, just the other day I found myself scouring my son's room for cash so I could settle up with a neighbor girl for one of those fundraiser coupon books I'd bought months ago[*] but still hadn't paid for. Needless to say, it's humbling when you owe a third-grader interest.

So since my two boys are starting to pay their own way (at least when it comes to luxury items like bowling balls and car insurance) I decided it's high time I show them there's no such thing as a free lunch (or road, or school, or library, or fire department, or parking lot, or whatever). Hence, I came

---

[*] And will never use.

up with "Federal Income Tax—the Home Edition." I sat them down and explained, "At the end of every quarter, we'll add up how much money you've made, and then you have to donate 10% of that to charity."

They looked at me like I'd just sprouted an alien out of my left eye.

"I don't understand," my younger finally questioned. "Are we in trouble?"

"No. But you have to understand that when you earn money, you don't get to keep it all."

"Why not? If you earned it, isn't it yours?"

"Well, yes, but someone's got to pay for all the common-usage stuff, and we have to put something away for people who fall on hard times."

My older son immediately understood the concept, since he started watching the national news just about the time Wall Street imploded. "Yeah," he said. "I get it. I'm in. How much?"

"Now wait a minute," the younger one argued. "We don't have any common-usage stuff in our house. So why do I have to pay for it?"

"Fine. Then every time you use the bathroom, you have to pay me a dollar. Also, I'll need to charge you to store your bike in the garage, and after every meal I'll present you with your food bill. Oh, and you can do your own laundry, but I'll have to charge you for the soap and water, and the use of the washer and dryer."

"Just pay the 10%," my older son whispered to his younger brother. "You're getting a deal."

"Or," I countered, "you could NOT work, but then you won't have money to do the things you want."

"Or you could just *give* me the money," the naïve, I mean younger, one shot back.

I narrowed my eyes, "Okay, that's fine by me. THAT will be the day you become my full-time maid, because you have to do *something* to earn you keep." I smiled sinisterly. "I cannot WAIT to show you how to fold my undies."

My son winced. "Um, what's the percentage I have to pay again?" he asked with total sincerity.

Last summer my older son made $751 mowing lawns, pet-sitting, and monitoring the chemicals in people's hot tubs. In September he bought a money order for $75 and made it out to one of our neighbors, a single mom who has a teenage son with cerebral palsy. The young man needed a new van that could accommodate his wheelchair, which his mother couldn't afford. So the community threw a fundraiser to help with the cost. My son, with little brother in tow, took the money order to my neighbor, who was delighted by his contribution.

Two things happened that day: one, both my kids finally understood why we have to pay taxes, and neither has since complained when I've requested they donate some of their own money to charity; and two, I felt fairly confident that neither of my boys would ever end up in the headline of some skanky tabloid because he came up short financially.

I think I'll go buy myself a nice, little expensive gift for those two small, but significant, parental accomplishments—right after I pay my taxes, of course.

Wipe, Wipe, Wipe My Memory Clean (of Those Annoying Kid Songs)

Last December, when our family did the annual search for the Christmas ornament boxes, it was hard not to notice that our basement had accumulated so much junk it was starting to look like an overpopulated Third World country. I swear there could be a whole colony of new life forms living down there, and I'd never know it.

As I meandered around the endless debris of mysterious, unmarked cardboard boxes, Halloween costumes, and Thomas the Tank Engine train tables (with infinite wooden track), I couldn't help but wonder, where the heck did all this stuff come from, and what happened to the days when I could fit everything I owned into the back of a 1975 VW Rabbit?

Finding the Christmas boxes took patience, which I ran

out of back in 2004, so I called in my 12-year-old son, to rummage around for any containers that when shaken sounded like either A) a jingle bell, or B) broken glass, in which case I think I might have finally found my missing wedding crystal. (I banished that impractical glassware shortly after we were married, because honestly, why would you let your tipsy guests drink out of fine crystal goblets when cheap wine glasses from World Market are so much easier to replace?)

As my son foraged through boxes of junk I did not recognize (a menorah? What the hell? We're not even Jewish!) I found a suitcase full of kid music videos on VHS tapes. Some of them I recalled, but most were as lost from memory as Cheerios in the couch cushions. (I'm guessing this was my brain's way of fighting back the monotony of hearing those same songs over and over. I choose to believe that over middle-aged memory loss.)

But one tape in particular caught my eye. And as soon as I saw it a song instantly sprang to mind. The video was *It's Potty Time,* and the song was "He's a Super Duper Pooper." And just like a nasty virus you can't shake, I went around the house the rest of the day with this touching lyric replaying in my head: *"He's a super duper pooper. He can potty with the best. No more diapers to get in the way, he can manage the rest."* Or something like that; I think I screwed up the last line, which makes me crazy because I can't stand it when people butcher song lyrics. I was 35 when I finally found out that Iron Butterfly's "In-A-Gadda-Da-Vita" was actually "In the Garden of Eden." Who knew? No one ever corrected me when I was 17. I was horrified to learn I'd been singing it wrong for the past 18 years. I mean, geez, what if it had come up in a job interview?

Anyway, by the time the *It's Potty Time* video reentered our lives technology had moved on. This just killed me because we didn't have a VHS player anymore, so I couldn't play the tape to relearn the song.

I tried to let it go, but then about an hour later, ANOTHER SONG from that stupid video bubbled up in my brain. It went something like this: *"Wipe, wipe, wipe yourself, always front to back...uh, merrily, merrily, merrily, merrily, life is but a dream."* No wait, that's not right. (Damn, this is going to drive me nuts.)

The more those song remnants romped around in my head like preschoolers on a sugar high, the more I began to think about my own childhood. Suddenly I thought, now wait a minute, do kids today really need to learn a whole new slate of mind-numbing toilet training tunes that will only take up valuable (and increasingly limited) memory when they're older? It was bad enough I had to endure nursery rhymes when I was little about babies falling out of treetops and some guy named Peter imprisoning his wife in a pumpkin shell. But at least I could sing those songs in mixed company when my mom paraded me around at family reunions. I mean, come on. Do you really want to be sitting in an Olive Garden when your kid busts a move with, *"On top of my potty, I'm sitting to poop. Your life is much better, when your diapers don't droop."* (Oh man, there's another latent *It's Potty Time* lyric that just invaded my head! Am I going to be able to get any sleep tonight?)

In retrospect, I don't know what I was thinking. I can't believe I had my sons learn songs about pooping. Me, the cool mom who sang Motown and Beatles' tunes to her babies instead of that sexist Mother Goose drivel. My kids knew the words to "I'll Be There" by the Jackson 5 and "When I'm Sixty-four" off the *Sergeant Pepper Lonely Hearts Club Band* album long before the video game *Rock Band* was even a flicker in some computer geek's head. And if I remember correctly (because it's all coming back to me now), somewhere in the *It's Potty Time* video there was even a male "fairy" (and I use that term loosely) playing a flute while a cute little girl was trying to make number two. Holy smokes, I'm surprised my boys weren't constipated until they were 10!

It's been months since the *It's Potty Time* video resurfaced, and believe it or not those song fragments still occasionally take up residence in my head like an outpost of termites hell-bent on colonizing the attic. I think my brain won't give up because it knows those lyrics are still in there somewhere between my high school boyfriend's middle name and the chemical element symbol for lead. A friend suggested I check to see if they're on iTunes or YouTube so I can finally resolve this and move on. Since everything ends up in cyberspace those melodies are probably out there somewhere, ready to remind anyone who stumbles upon them, *"This is the way we wash our hands after we go to the pah-tee."* (Dang, there's another one.)

The Science of Common Sense

Recently I was asked to be a science fair judge at our local elementary school. Even though my kids have graduated from said school, the PTO over there knows a sucker when they see one. And that would be me.

Seems the school had trouble recruiting volunteer judges because they held the proctoring from noon to two. Call me crazy, but if you want to maximize your parent volunteers you don't ask them to give up that precious time when their kids are in school. Don't get me wrong, we all love our children more than life itself. But you have to admit, whether you're running a Fortune 500 company or running the dishwasher, you get way more done when the kids are off learning how to conjugate verbs and factor polynomials five days a week.

Having two boys three years apart, I spent NINE YEARS

as a volunteer at that elementary school. Even though I've moved on to the exciting world of junior high and high school, I'm pretty sure the masterminds at the elementary still have my number programmed into the *This-Parent-is-Too-Wimpy-to-Say-No* section of their phone system. I bet I have my own speed-dial button and everything.

Which reminds me, I need to seriously think about changing my contact info—and possibly my identity—if I want to ensure my future success in the School Volunteer Witness Protection Program. I know many high school moms who went through this program, and as a result they now look nothing like they did when their kids were little. For one thing, they comb their hair and shower more often. They don't walk around with spittle or other bodily fluids dripping down their shirts. And every one of them can complete a sentence without interjecting, "Do you have to go potty?", "Don't make me stop this car!", or "Get your hand out of your pants." (Oh, wait, that last one was directed at the dads. Never mind.) The really hard-core volunteer moms who want out (i.e. room mothers) have been known to lose weight, color their hair, and even learn a foreign language (or take on a phony accent) just to help hide their identities. However, you know they've completely crossed over when they stop buying their underwear at Walmart. At that point it becomes poignant.

But until I get up the nerve to actually join this program, how can I say no to third-graders and their baking soda-and-vinegar volcanoes? So off I went to judge the elementary school science fair.

And because I'm such a softie, I vowed to be a just, but lenient, judge. Far be it from me to spoil some child's dream of becoming the next Madame Curie or Carl Sagan. I mean, after all, I don't want to toot my own horn, but (ahem) I did major in math back in the *I-am-woman-hear-me-roar* days when very few girls went into the hard sciences. I have to admit, it wasn't the most exciting of majors. However, it was dominated by males, so the dating pool was huge—if you liked *Star Wars* fan boys who preferred typing FORTRAN punch cards over getting hammered at the Delta Chi House on Friday nights (which I did—preferred the geeks over Greeks, I mean).

So suffice it to say I felt qualified to judge an elementary school science fair. That is, until I came upon my first project: a Play-Doh diorama of how the linear accelerator at Stanford University splits an atom—presented by Billy, age 10.

I'm sorry, but who let this kid in here? His parents obviously did his project for him. So I asked, "Billy, what is your hypothesis?"

"Is a particle accelerator more efficient if it runs straight or in a circle?" he replied.

"If you have to ask, then I'd say you didn't do your homework, young man."

"No, that's my hypothesis. There's some debate over

whether or not a linear accelerator can justify its cost over its traditional circular counterpart. I think it can."

"Oh. And you're going to prove that with Play-Doh?"

"Yes." The kid then proceeded to talk for 10 minutes using words like *antimatter, cold cathode, radio frequency,* and *protons.* I nodded pensively, even though I had no idea what the hell he was talking about.

When he was finished he looked at me proudly, like he'd just unlocked the secrets of the universe (and for all I know, he had). Suddenly I realized he wanted me to speak. "Um, I like your shoes. Did you get those at the Famous Footwear factory outlet?"

"Is that...part of your evaluation?" he asked, sensing I was about as scientific as wood.

"No. I'm killing time until I can think of something intelligent to say, so I don't look like a goober in front of someone who's younger than the mold in my refrigerator." (Now there's a science project.) Actually, I didn't say that. Instead I asked him why he thought we needed a particle accelerator in the first place.

"Well... Uh... Because... it's cool?" he sheepishly replied.

I just stared at this kid for a moment, and then it hit me. He knew all about the technology of a particle accelerator (meaning *how it worked*), but he didn't know *why* someone would bother to build it in the first place.

Einstein once said, "Logic will get you from A to B. Imagination will take you everywhere." With the Internet and all kinds of Wikis available to anyone who can aimlessly punch a keyboard like a monkey throwing darts, a kid has access to more information than our parents ever learned in their lifetimes. But is it enough to just know stuff? Isn't it equally (if not more) important to know what to do with the stuff we learn?

Suddenly I was back in the driver's seat.

"So if a particle accelerator is more efficient when it shoots particles in a straight line, as opposed to a circle, what does that buy you?" I asked with all the confidence of Yoda.

He looked at me like I'd unexpectedly put his king in check. Actually, he'd already answered my question during his dissertation on linear accelerators, but he was so focused on the "wow, gee-whiz" aspect of the technology, he didn't realize he'd given me the "We need it because…" part. After eight seconds of uncomfortable silence, I told him to think about *why* you'd want to move particles around really fast (in circles or a straight line), and that I'd come back in a minute to see what he came up with.

In the meantime, I went to the drinking fountain and threw cold water on my face. I get uncomfortably sweaty when intellectually challenged by fifth-graders. I mean, this little scientific exchange turned out okay, but I had to be on my toes to come out on top *this time*. Honestly, I hadn't planned on having to think that hard, and justifying the existence of particle accelerators was not on my short list of things to do that day.

I took a deep breath and moved on to the next project, done by a cute little blond girl with braids and bright pink nail polish. "Okay, what have you got for me?" I asked.

"Using Einstein's Theory of Relativity I am going to prove that time travel is possible," she said with a lisp through her two missing front teeth.

Holy Mother of Sweet Pickles, you've got to be kidding me! Where the heck are the baking soda volcanoes?

"Um, would you excuse me for just a minute, sweetheart?" I scurried off with my tail between my legs to find the science fair parent organizer, who happened to hiding out in the teachers' lounge watching *The World's Dumbest Hunting Accidents* on YouTube.

"Okay, it's official. We're just a pack of prehistoric posers when it comes to technology," I said as I watched some hayseed blow his toe off with a shotgun.

"What are you talking about?" she answered. "You have a math degree." I looked at her suspiciously. "Hey, we do background checks on all our science fair judges. You should see what we go through just to approve our safety patrol volunteers."

"It doesn't matter. That math degree is over 25 years old. Kids don't need science fairs to learn math and science.

Information is everywhere. They just have to surf the Web. Our kids are technology natives. We're just immigrants at best." I sighed. "Maybe I should move on. Maybe *it is* time I applied to the Volunteer Witness Protection Program."

"I don't think so."

"Why not?"

"Because last I checked the Internet has a long way to go before it can teach a child common sense." We both looked at the computer screen just in time to see a reenactment of Dick Cheney shooting his friend in the face.

Damn. Now I was the one backed into a corner. Even before I walked in there like the class crumb bum who thought she could skate through this *easy* assignment, I knew in my heart it was my duty to stay in the game...at least until my kids are out of school or my brain turns to mush—whichever comes first.

Volunteering for anything is important, but volunteering to make the next generation better than the previous one is essential, even if it means dragging out brain cells that haven't been used in years and risking looking like a dimwitted goober in the process. (Crap, it's junior high all over again.)

We mistakenly believe that technology makes kids smarter, but in reality it sometimes does just the opposite. Left to its own devices technology simply spoon-feeds our kids "fun facts" without supplying the cognitive tissue to put it all together into something meaningful (or at the very least, useful). Which is why teachers, mentors, counselors, tutors, school administrators, advisors, and even middle-aged parents with 25-year-old math degrees will never go out of style.

I sighed, suddenly feeling very melancholy over the passing of the baking soda-and-vinegar volcanoes. But at the same time I realized that science fairs aren't outdated at all. In fact they are needed now more than ever.

And so with great pride (and more than a little fear) I turned my back on the mindless YouTube videos blaring from my friend's computer screen and dutifully walked back into the gym to finish judging the *imperative* elementary school science fair.

The Name of the Game

The other day I went into my 12-year-old son's room to ask him a question and found him and his buddy glued to a 17-inch computer flat screen while they maneuvered joysticks with the precision of fighter pilots. They were so intent on collecting rubies (while avoiding land mines) in the latest iteration of that oldie, but goodie, *The Legend of Zelda* that real bombs could have gone off around them and they wouldn't have noticed.

"Have you seen the good scissors?" I asked.

"Huh?" said my artistically gifted son with the intelligence of a tree stump.

"The good scissors. I need them to cut off your brother's head." I replied, testing his comprehension.

"In a minute, Mom. I still have a little life left."

"Well, hurry up and kill yourself so we can have a normal conversation!" Now there's a sentence I never thought I'd say in my lifetime.

As I watched my son and his friend do battle with evil trolls and other vermin of the underworld, I thought to myself, how did we come to this? What did kids do before video games? What *did I* do when I was a kid? How *did I* spend my time with my friends? I had plenty of time to soul-search since my son and his friend suddenly found a bottle of life potion, so now they were nowhere near ending their game.

*   *   *   *

Last December we found ourselves as a family at a local mall drooling over Christmas gifts we couldn't afford *and* searching for a wedding gift for a friend who was going on her fourth marriage come New Year's Eve. Since she'd already built up her household three times and was the recipient of multiple alimony checks, she was rather hard to shop for. I mean, what do you get the woman who has already *taken* everything?

"I know," said tween son, "let's get her some video games."

"But she doesn't have any kids," I replied, and thankfully so, I added to myself.

"Which means we could get her the *really good* games!" He replied, eyeing the latest edition of *Call of Duty*. (How the heck is it that we always end up in the electronics department of any store we visit?)

Giving up on the weird kitchen appliances (ginger slicer, anyone?) and gaudy crystal candy dishes, I followed my kids to the toy department, where we meandered around until we found ourselves in the game aisle.

"Boring!" my younger son sang. "Where are the iPads?"

"Now, hold on there, look at this." In the middle of the aisle I found a lonely demonstration copy of the board game Battleship set up for anyone to play. I loved this game as a kid and quickly explained to my children how you play it. They said it sounded too easy to be fun, but agreed to humor me until one of us sunk one of the others' battleships.

After just a few guesses, my kids actually found one of my battleships, and they were so excited you'd think they'd discovered my secret hiding place for chocolate (it's in the toolshed, but don't tell them). We continued playing, laughing and barking out coordinates like a family of demented bingo players. Soon other kids gathered round and watched intently, occasionally joining in by shouting out a spontaneous "B 20!"

It took almost a half hour of this playful banter before it finally hit me. *Now* I remember what I did with my friends when I was little. We played games. Not just made-up games, but board games, card games, even dice games. (Remember Yahtzee?) How could I have forgotten about my beloved Monopoly? One game could go an entire season.

    *   *   *   *

I grew up in a typical, dysfunctional, mid-twentieth century family. The adults fought like rabid dogs, and none of us really had anything in common except for our love of games. We never planned a family game night, it always just kind of happened on its own whenever it needed to. Back then there were only three network TV stations, and no cable or satellite TV, no VCRs, DVDs, DVRs, Netflix, YouTube, Hulu, Apple TV, smartphones, or video games. Like me, television programming was still in its childhood (meaning it was pretty immature), so we never considered planning our lives around it. But we did plan our evenings around Clue, Tripoli, chess, canasta, and Parcheesi. Playing games was the one thing that brought us together, even though as a family we were about as functional as a broken clock. We could never agree on anything, except that I always got to be Mrs. Peacock (in Clue), and my sister always got to be the boot (in Monopoly).

Even though my own family now doesn't suffer from the same dysfunctionalities I endured as a kid (we've developed our own, unique brand, thank you very much), I decided it was time to start the tradition of games with my own brood. In the last few years my sons have learned the joys of Operation, Scrabble, Uno, Euchre, Life, Trouble, Sorry, Pictionary, Yahtzee, Monopoly, a variety of rummy card games, and of course Battleship (which, by the way, is great on airplane trips). And just like when I was a kid, family game night at our house evolves organically whenever it needs to.

Part of the joy of sharing my love of games with my kids is watching them share that same enthusiasm with their friends.

"Do you like cribbage?" my son once asked a buddy.

"No," replied his friend. "It gives me gas."

I just sat back and enjoyed the puzzled look on my son's face.

In retrospect, our kids want to know why we didn't come clean about games sooner, but honestly, I didn't think Shoots and Ladders stood a chance against Homer Simpson popping out of an Xbox 360.

Apparently I was wrong.

My Christmas Gift

Last year I got the most unexpected of Christmas presents. Something I didn't even ask for, and in fact, didn't even want. I got a lovely holiday hernia, complete with a purple bulge next to my belly button and more pain than if the baby Jesus Himself had risen up out of his nativity scene and socked me in the gut. And because a hernia is the gift that keeps on giving, I got the wonderful follow-up gift of hernia surgery three days after Christmas.

I don't think the universe was paying much attention to what I really wanted for Christmas, which was the ability to eat buckets of French fries and chocolate-covered potato chips without my cholesterol shooting up high enough to give a buffalo a heart attack, and boobs that don't sag into my armpits when I lie on my back. Jesus, is that too much to ask?

Literally, Jesus, I'm asking you.

Anyway, exactly one week before Christmas I bent over to pick up a box and suddenly felt like I was stabbed in the gut with a hot knife. I'd just been to a coffee shop and thought, "Damn, that waitress gave me milk when I specifically asked for a soy latte." Yes, I thought it was just gas pains due to my lactose intolerance, so I bravely ignored the fact that by the end of the day the pain got so intense I broke out into a cold sweat and became increasingly nauseous. "Man, that must have been *whole milk*," I thought.

I suffered through the weekend before Christmas, wondering why my stomach felt the need to antagonize me, until finally I went to the doctor on the following Tuesday. My doctor took one look at the hard, purple knob next to my belly button (which I thought was just a bruise from God knows what—the whole milk, maybe) and told me that I had a strangulated hernia and that I needed to go to the local hospital and have a surgeon look at it *now*!

What? It's three days before Christmas! I have people coming in from out of town tomorrow, I haven't finished my Christmas shopping, and the bathroom looks like the climactic scene of *Invasion of the Body Snatchers* (just before the moldy pod spores come to life—cue the music). Not to mention I'd just bought an expensive organic ham for Christmas dinner, and that little piggy certainly wasn't going to cook itself. This was simply unacceptable.

The surgeon (a nice lady who thought getting rid of a painful and potentially dangerous hernia *before* Christmas was a smart idea) said she could operate on me the next day (which was two days before Christmas). I begged her to take a second look to make sure it *really was* some vital organ that was trying to escape my abdominal cavity and not a whole-milk bruise (given the chance, I'll blame dairy for anything). Because if my stomach wasn't actually trying to make a break for it I would much rather put the surgery off until Monday. That way I could enjoy Christmas knowing that I wouldn't have to be the one to take down the tree and figure out how to repack a bunch of ornaments in boxes that seemed too small and too few to fit all the Christmas doodads we'd accumulated over the years. (Can someone please tell me how we ended up with an ornament that says "Baby's first Christmas" for the year 1997 when neither of my kids was born that year? And why, for heaven's sake, is it pink when I only have boys?)

The surgeon said she could examine me further, but that she'd have to poke and prod my belly, causing me more pain than listening to Glenn Beck and Sean Hannity pontificate on universal health care in stereo. I told her, "Bring it on, sister!" Anything to ensure my husband didn't get the chance to ruin my holiday ham.

Well, needless to say, in the few minutes (probably seconds, but it felt like minutes) that she kneaded my belly like Silly Putty, I decided I hated her. She kept apologizing for causing such pain, and finally stopped when she noticed my face frozen in an expression that looked like the mask from the movie *Scream*.

"You're right," my doctor conceded. "It's not attached to an organ. It's just a little pocket of abdominal fat that broke through a tear in your stomach muscle wall. If you can stand the pain over the weekend, we can wait until Monday to fix it."

Excuse me, but I didn't hear anything after the words *abdominal fat*. What do you mean, abdominal fat? I lift weights at least once a week—okay, once a month (all right, so maybe it's more like once a year). And I run the equivalent of three miles a day…if you were to add up all the movement I do in between sitting. And now you're telling me that in addition to preventing me from fitting into my skinny jeans during certain times of the month, my abdominal fat is causing me to have major surgery just days before the end of the year, even though I haven't met my deductible? How is that possible?

"Welcome to middle-age," she said matter-of-factly. "All that stuff you did when you were young, well, it's finally catching up with you."

"You mean like…what? Having kids?"

"I was thinking more along the lines of ski accidents or old, sorority-pledge week injuries, but yeah, being a human

U-Haul for 40 weeks twice in a lifetime does eventually take its toll."

"Wait, are you saying my kids gave me a hernia?" I asked.

"Heavens, no. It could've been anything from doing the hustle at a '70s revival dance to a hearty sneeze. At your age it's hard to tell." Somehow that didn't exactly make me feel any better. "I'll schedule your surgery for Monday. Recovery will take four to six weeks."

"What?" I wailed. "So now my abdominal fat is going to ruin my New Year's Eve, too? What the hell? Since when did my abdominal fat get to be the boss of me?"

"When it started leaking out of a hole in your stomach wall," my doctor deadpanned. "See you Monday. In the meantime, have a holly, jolly Christmas, don't lift anything, and here's a prescription for some painkillers." (FINALLY some good news.)

I didn't lift anything all weekend. In fact, it was the perfect excuse to get everyone to do everything for me while I gave directives on exactly how it all should be done. It wasn't much different from regular life, except now I was on doctor's orders to be bossy (okay, so I stretched it a little, but hey, they all bought into it). Ironically, this turned out to be the best Christmas ever. Nothing like a little holiday hernia to bring a family together.

But my New Year's Eve, on the other hand, was a royal

pain in the gut. By a week later all the really good surgery drugs had worn off. The new painkillers I was on made me nauseous, so I switched to ones that weren't quite as strong. Now I could stand up without rocking back and forth like a Weeble, but my stomach hurt so badly that I walked all hunched over like a little, old lady in search of loose change on West Palm Beach.

Of course, this was the year we just happened to be invited to *six million* different New Year's Eve parties. For decades we sat home on New Year's Eve doing nothing because A) we couldn't get a sitter, or B) we weren't invited to anyone's party, or C) we were too cheap to pay to go to one of those restaurant shindigs for pathetic people who don't get invited to real New Year's Eve parties.

But now that our kids were old enough to babysit themselves we didn't have to acknowledge their existence if we wanted to go to a neighbor's house to do an inebriated hokey-pokey with lampshades on our heads. So when some good friends invited us over to their house for a night of raucous fun, and by the way, bring the kids (they had teenagers, too), of course my family conveniently forgot I had stitches in my tummy.

When I reminded them I couldn't go, they all stopped jumping for joy just long enough to get panicked looks on their faces. "But I think you guys should go to the party anyway, without me," I offered.

I assumed they heard me because they were out the door before I finished my sentence.

But that's okay, because the punch line of this story is that my diabolical plan worked. While they were out whooping it up I was home alone in a quiet house reading a book by the fire. No one asked me why they didn't have clean underwear. No one announced that the toilet had overflowed. And no one turned up Lenny Picket so loud that I thought Tower of Power had reunited and actually stopped by to play a set. (Did I mention it was quiet?)

I knew they'd all be out until at least midnight, so I read and watched TV until 11:30 and then went to bed. I never heard them come in. Yep, it was the nicest, *quietest* New Year's Eve a hernia could ever give you.

And I'm not ashamed to say I loved every second of it.

Working Off Fat Season

Recently I started going to the gym. I've never been one for exercising indoors, but when you live at 7,000 feet winter lasts a good seven months, and by May you're so sick of snow (and being cold) you want to bitch-slap Mother Nature with an icicle. Believe me, it just doesn't feel right to be outside jogging in weather that makes your nose hairs freeze.

Also by May you notice the effects of what I call "Fat Season" peaking out in the form of unsightly dimples on your thighs, or the ever-so-slight beginnings of a muffin top bulging out over the yoga pants you comfortably wore all last summer (I don't do yoga, I just love the pants). Fat Season encompasses the months in which you consume so many sweets and so much rich food you start to convince yourself that "junk" is a new food group.

These wretched few months start in October with Halloween, then continue through Thanksgiving, Christmas, Valentine's Day, Easter, and end with Mother's Day, which is just about when you put on a pair of shorts for the first time in six months and realize your skin is even paler and lumpier than you remember it being last Labor Day. And by the way, at what point during the winter did I suddenly acquire the belly of a spayed puma? (That one really snuck up on me.) All I can say is thank God for turtlenecks that go all the way down to your knees.

So it was time to hit the gym.

Even though I like everyone to believe that I started working out (again) to improve my health, the reality is I re-upped my gym membership because I had nothing else to do at 6:00 in the morning. You see, my teenage son has a zero-hour varsity jazz band class at his high school at 6:30 a.m. Since he can't drive yet, and I don't want him walking to school in the dark carrying an overloaded backpack that contains a variety of heavy woodwinds, I have to get up and take him to school just before the sun rises. And once I'm up, I can't go back to sleep. I tried writing during that time, but when I reviewed my work hours later I concluded that the side of my brain that produces crappy prose is an early riser while the creative side likes to sleep late.

Knowing this, I decided to work on my physical being instead. So I went to the gym, parked my flabby fanny on a stationary bike, and just hoped that the contact of my flannel sweat pants with the Naugahyde bike seat would cause some sort of chemical reaction that miraculously resulted in a firmer butt. I mean, isn't that how exercise works? It's been so long, I really don't know.

But as suspected I soon got bored with the stationary bike and graduated to the elliptical, on which I also did a whole lot of moving without getting anywhere. Honestly, what's the point of exerting so much energy if you stay in the same spot? I really don't get it. Yes, I know this equipment works your cardiovascular system, but what good is a healthy heart if you go insane from boredom? Do we really need that many fit, crazy people running around? At least on an outdoor bike ride there's stuff to look at (as opposed to that sweaty, fat guy in loose shorts who does Pilates poses over a big, rubber fitness ball—yeah, that's a pleasant way to start my day). No matter which stationery bike I ride at the gym I'm forced to stare (if I don't want to look at Sweaty Pilates Guy) at the indoor tennis courts, where I have to watch people having fun doing *real* exercise.

After a couple of weeks of this nonsense I decided to get off the human hamster wheel and hit the weight room instead. Being there at 6:00 in the morning I figured I'd have the place all to myself and thus wouldn't have to feel wimpy about using the small weights usually reserved for stroke victims and skinny eighth-grade boys trying to move up a weight class on the wrestling team.

How wrong I was.

Apparently, six in the morning is the new happy hour for the bridge-and-tunnel crowd. Gym rats of all sorts work out before heading off to the office, but in doing so they also strut around the facilities like a gaggle of peacocks in heat. One guy drew attention to himself by grunting so much when he lifted his gargantuan, 50-lb. weights that he sounded like he was either having a heart attack or taking a really big poop. Either way, I didn't want any part of it.

When I moved to the other side of the room I found myself next to a forty-something woman with an incredible body. I won't even say "for her age" because she was so firm she made Michael Phelps look like a flabby couch potato. I swear to God, that woman could crack Brazil nuts between her butt cheeks. Yet every time she lifted her overloaded barbell she let out a rather "climactic" moan usually reserved for the privacy of one's own bedroom (or in my case, when I first step into a nice hot shower or take a bite of dark chocolate).

Then there's the geeky dude who'll hit on anything, including a middle-aged mom who's there only because she had to drop her kid off at school at six in the morning and has nothing better to do before her middle-schooler has to get up at 7:30. ("Uh, thanks, but no thanks. I've already seen K.C. and the Sunshine Band in concert—twice.")

Clearly, I'm out of my league if I want to go to the weight room at dawn. They need a sign above the door that says, "You must be divorced or single to enter between the hours of 6:00 and 8:00 a.m." Since I'm neither, I decided to come back later.

But in the meantime I drove around until I found an open Starbucks, where I ordered a double soy latte and a Heath Bar pastry. I actually thought the sign said "Health Bar," which is why I bought two. However, after I'd taken the first bite I instantly knew I'd made a mistake. Nothing that yummy could be healthy. And since the cashier wouldn't let me return either one, I had no choice but to eat them—all 2,400 calories. Oh well. Fortunately, Fat Season isn't officially over until the day after Mother's Day. Until then I'll just wear my body-length turtleneck and avoid the gym at all costs.

Humbled By a Gnome, Forgiven By a Stranger

Last year on his fifteenth birthday I took my eldest son to the DMV, where he promptly received his driver's permit. As I watched the lady behind the counter give my son his new credential my hair instantly turned three shades whiter, and the lines on my face dug in a little deeper. It hadn't hit me until he actually had his permit in hand that he was now legally allowed to get behind the wheel of a car and potentially cause accidents for which my husband and I would be held responsible. Plus, our insurance was about to triple for the privilege. Ah, yes. What a momentous day.

The fun started as soon as we exited the DMV and headed for the car. Apparently, he was a changed man from when we first got there, because now that he had his permit he miraculously knew how to operate a motor vehicle well enough to drive from Heber to Park City, which included a 20-minute trip on a freeway. Forget the fact that when we walked into the DMV just an hour or so before literally he didn't know how to turn on the windshield wipers.

"Can I drive?" he asked confidently.

I kept a straight face even though in my head hilarity ensued. It took all my strength not to come back with, "Sure you can drive, when donkeys play professional poker and they let pigs join the Olympic Curling Team... When your brother becomes a urinary sharpshooter and they make a toilet seat that cleans itself... When the dogs can vacuum up their own hairballs and do our taxes..." I actually had to take a moment to let the one-liners in my vivid imagination die down before I politely uttered, "Um, well...my car has a manual transmission."

"Yeah, so?"

"I hate to point out the obvious, but you've never driven a stick shift before."

Even though my son had just turned 15 that day, his actual first time behind the wheel of a car was on his fourteenth birthday. All he wanted that year in the way of a gift was to learn how to drive, so we took him to a huge, deserted parking lot on a Sunday and gave him a crash course (no pun intended) on how to drive our bulbous 1998 Mazda MPV, which just happened to have an automatic transmission.

Twenty minutes into it, however, when he got *drive* and *reverse* mixed up and almost hit the lamppost in front of him while trying to *back out* of a parking spot, I promptly ended the lesson due to my sweaty armpits and jangled nerves.

We made a few more attempts throughout the year, but never got beyond parking lots and my sister's rural acreage (on which he drove my brother-in-law's Bobcat tractor). So suffice it to say he knew as much about driving as Mother Teresa knew about being the grand marshal at a Mardi Gras parade.

But that was a moot point, as far as he was concerned. "I've watched you drive a stick, so I know how to do it," he declared.

On the one hand I was proud of his confidence, on the other hand I was terrified of his ignorance. "Tell you what, I'll drive home, but when we get there I'll let you try out this car in the neighborhood church parking lot. (Thank God for parking lots. I never really knew how handy they were until I had a teenager learning to drive.)

"But that's so small," he protested. "Why can't I go out on the road?"

"Let's see if you can just get the car to go two feet first," I countered, "and then we'll talk about taking it out on the road."

He rolled his eyes and shook his head as if *I* were the unreasonable child. That's okay, I thought. We'll see how much his head shakes when he chokes the engine to death just trying to go forward in first gear. For good measure I stopped at home and picked up his 12-year-old brother, who was more than happy to sit in the back seat and offer colorful commentary.

When we got to the parking lot I demonstrated as I explained to my son how you had to simultaneously give the car a little gas as you slowly let out the clutch. To his credit, he listened carefully, nodded assuredly, and waited until I was done talking before he asked if we could switch seats so he could try it. He was so fearless about the whole idea of driving a stick he actually had me convinced that he *just might* know what he was doing.

We quickly did the clown-car shuffle, which ended with him in the driver seat and me riding shotgun. "Okay, let's go," I said without a hint of worry in my voice.

He put on his seatbelt, boldly released the parking brake, and then with all the confidence of a rock star gave it some gas and then promptly killed the engine, but not before it bucked twice, like a dying man taking his last gasps of air.

Little brother laughed so hard from the back seat he had tears in his eyes. "That was just like Mr. Toad's Wild Ride...only wilder!" he announced. "I think we actually left the ground! Can we do it again?"

"I think there's something wrong with this car," my older son said sincerely, ignoring his bothersome younger brother.

"There's nothing wrong with the car," I assured him.

"Well, it doesn't do that when you drive it," he reasoned.

"No, and it never will. You just have to learn how to time it right."

"Can I try?" my 12-year-old asked, poking his head up front in between the bucket seats. "I know I can do *way* better than him!"

"No, you can't drive. You're only 12."

"So? I can reach the pedals, if that's what you're worried about."

"I know you might find this hard to believe, but *that* is not my biggest concern when it comes to putting you behind the wheel." I turned my attention back to the son who *was* behind the wheel. "Okay, this time give it a little more gas while you're releasing the clutch. You might hear the engine rev at first, but…" I didn't get to finish my sentence because suddenly we zoomed forward from zero to 50 in a New York *second*. But then just as quickly the car gasped to a stop when he took his feet off all the pedals.

Little brother was now laughing so hard he was on the verge of wetting his pants.

This game of repeated whiplash continued a few more times until my son finally started the car smoothly and got it up to 20 mph, at which time the engine revved so loudly it sounded like a swarm of angry hornets.

"What do I do now?" he asked as he drove in circles, just so he could keep his speed up.

"Put the clutch in and shift into second." He did, and the car violently pitched forward, but by gosh, he successfully got it into second gear. So now we were going in circles *even faster*.

After about 45 minutes of jolting from first to second, back down to first, and then back into second, I suggested we go out on the neighborhood roads, not because I thought he was ready, but because I was so carsick from driving in circles I thought I might blow chunks all over my heated leather seats.

He carefully pulled out onto the residential street, which was the first time he'd driven on public property. This is it, I thought. We are now officially *liable*. Oh dear Lord, I silently prayed, please don't let us encounter any other moving vehicles while we're out here. (Funny how I'm never religious except when I need a really big favor. Then I don't know if it's so much religious as it is desperate.) Well, apparently God wasn't listening, either that or He has an incredibly dark sense of humor. Because coming right at us on a narrow street that was barely big enough for two horses to pass each other was a huge construction truck with a load of gravel. And of course, it was going way too fast.

"Oh, shit," I muttered under my breath.

"Uh, Mom?"

"Yes, I see it. Just get over as far to the right as you can. NOW." He did, and that's when I noticed we were heading straight for a parked car. Damn these neighbors and their visiting friends. Why do they have to be so social right at the moment my kid is learning to drive? Don't they know we need every inch of road space during these nerve-racking lessons?

"Okay, you need to slow down, or better yet, STOP."

"When?"

"Now would be good," I quickly replied, as I repeatedly pumped the invisible passenger-side brake Subaru had so thoughtlessly forgotten to install.

"Are we going to hit that car?" my 12-year-old asked excitedly.

"Stop it, NOW!"

"Who? Him or me?" my surprisingly calm older son asked.

"Both of you! ESPECIALLY YOU!" I clarified to the kid behind the wheel.

He immediately stomped on a pedal, but we kept gliding forward. "That's the clutch! Hit the brake! Hit the brake!" I yelled with the intensity of an air-raid siren.

He danced over all the pedals with both feet like he was doing a maniacal Irish jig until the engine mercifully cut out about a foot behind the parked car.

As the truck sailed by the friendly driver gave us a thank-you wave for letting him pass. I felt like flipping the guy off, but thought better of it since I knew he'd be totally confused by the gesture. (Plus, my kids were in the car and I try to limit my instinctive crazy-lady persona as much as possible when they're around. By the way, that plan's not working out so well the older they get.)

We all sat quietly for a second until my older son finally broke the silence with, "I guess I didn't do so well." I looked at him; sincere defeat hung on his face. I wanted to gloat, "I told you so," but I couldn't bring myself to do it because the situation was all too familiar.

When I was just a couple of years older than him I learned to drive a stick by practicing in my parents' long driveway in Oakland, California, back and forth, never getting above second gear (my version of a parking lot). Until one day I finally got cocky and decided to venture out into the neighborhood all by myself (after all I'd had my license by then for two years, for pity's sake).

Within minutes of being on public streets I hit a trash can, which knocked over a metal rake, which hit the ugliest lawn gnome ever to grace the planet. The rake broke off the gnome's hand, except for its thumb, which because of the angle made it look like he was giving the neighborhood the bird. So now, in addition to being hideous, he was also incredibly rude.

Panic flooded over me. I wasn't sure what to do. What if I just left? Could I be put in jail for hit-and-run of a gnome? I looked around for witnesses.

Even though I didn't see anyone, common sense took over, and I sheepishly went up to the front door to confess my crime. Thankfully, no one was home. I thought about writing a note, but as I was a cash-strapped college student at the time, I didn't relish the thought of paying to replace this repulsive inanimate creature (which actually had more character now that he was minus four fingers).

Just as I was about to make a run for it, a car pulled into the driveway. A man got out, looked at the gnome, and then looked at me. "Did you do this?" he asked.

I felt like a cornered fugitive. "Yes," I confessed. "I'm so sorry. I'm learning to drive a stick, and I…" I paused, not wanting to admit that I momentarily forgot how to stop the car. "I promise I'll pay for a new one."

"Are you kidding? I should pay you. I hate that thing." He looked at it. "Is it flipping me off?" I didn't know what to say, so I didn't say anything. "My wife bought it in Mexico. But now I think we have a really good reason to um… *retire him*." He picked up the revolting statue and tossed it in the trash can. "Don't worry about it." He then walked into his house, and I never saw him again.

I checked my parents' car for damage, but the trash can left only a dusty mark that I easily brushed away. So after giving it a lot of thought (in a matter of 20 seconds) I decided not to tell my parents. They never knew. Until now. When they read this. (Surprise!)

Humbled by a gnome, forgiven by a stranger.

I looked at my son and saw immediately that my ordinary four-wheel-drive wagon had similarly bitch-slapped my little boy down from his own teenage bravado to a self-doubting greenhorn. Not the first (or last) of many lessons he was destined to learn just by giving it a shot…and failing. He didn't need me telling him he sucked at driving a stick.

"Well, your first attempt was better than mine," I told him truthfully.

"At least you didn't hit that car," my younger son rationalized.

Or a gnome, I thought.

"You'll get it." I told him. "It just takes practice…which we will save for another day. An hour of this is about all I'm good for."

"Okay," he said sheepishly. He turned the key in the ignition, only to have the car leap forward like a spooked thoroughbred. The gap between our bumper and the car in front of us instantly narrowed by about six inches.

I took a deep, cleansing breath. "You have to put the clutch in when…"

"Yeah, yeah. I know." He turned on the car, put it in reverse and jerked backward.

After we drove for about a block my blood pressure started to return to normal, and I suddenly remembered something else about my encounter with the gnome. Even though I received a pardon, I was intimidated by the evil stick shift and didn't want to drive again *ever*. Eventually, I got over it, but not before I beat myself up.

"Turn left up here," I told my son.

"Why?" he asked. "I thought we were done."

"I've changed my mind," I said, taking another deep inhalation. "I think we should take the long way home."

A Parent's Summer Vacation

By the time there are only five weeks of school left before summer vacation begins I find myself glancing at the calendar A LOT. Not that I'm counting. I just like looking at the calendar—and mentally counting down the days until I get a 10-week pardon from being the resident homework harpy and official family chauffer.

As with anything you look forward to, the anticipation of summer vacation is better than the vacation itself. When I was a kid we started the countdown the day after spring break ended. Whether you liked school or not, it was a betrayal of childhood if you didn't curse those last two and a half months of academic incarceration.

Now that I'm a parent I still look forward to summer vacation…sort of. I work at home, so I'm not thrilled by the idea of having my little munchkins constantly ask me what time it is (when they can all read a clock); or can I make them a sandwich (even though their arms aren't broken); or can they make a parachute and jump off the roof to see if it works like it did on *Mythbusters* (hey, at least they asked first).

However, there are parental perks to summer vacation, the biggest one being (as I said earlier, but it bears repeating) the reprieve from homework. No longer do I have the routine debate with a middle-schooler about how to pronounce spelling words like *defibrillator* and *corps*. Nor do I have to negotiate exactly *when* he'll get his homework done. I'd like him to get it out of the way immediately after he comes home from school, but of course, he'd rather wait until right before bed, because you know, why do it earlier when you could be practicing your bassoon instead.

And once school's out for the summer, my job as designated driver for Mom's Taxi Service decreases substantially. Gone are the band concerts, multiple music lessons, orthodontist appointments, pep rallies, play practices, science fairs, football and basketball games to which I'm expected to shuttle everyone, sometimes with the dilemma of having to be in two places at once. (Okay, so we still have the orthodontist gig in the summer, but that's relatively mild compared to the rest.) Fortunately, our town provides free public bus service (worth every penny of local tax money, I might add). So if my kids want to spend a summer afternoon at the skateboard park or the dirt bike track, they can darn well get there on their own. I really don't care what they do during the months of June, July, and August as long as it's A) not illegal, B) not harmful, and C) I don't have to drive them.

Yes, summer vacation is a mixed bag for me, but I have a summer vacation fantasy that outweighs anything you'd ever read in a trashy novel. It goes like this: Every morning I awaken to the sound of the cappuccino machine hissing in the kitchen (but not before 8:00) as my children blend the perfect soy latte. They bring it to me in bed, along with a warm chocolate croissant, *The New York Times*, and my laptop so that I may check e-mail, Twitter, and Facebook, and work on my Great American Novel in the comfort of a king-size bed that I have all to myself.

When I finally emerge, I enter a kitchen that has already been cleaned up from the nutritious breakfast my dear, sweet children prepared for themselves. The pets have been fed, all beds have been made, teeth have been brushed, kids are dressed, and everyone stands in line to kiss Mom and wish her a wonderful day, just as they go out the door for play dates (my boys cringe when I still use that term; "It's *hanging out*, Mom.") they arranged themselves, which means they will be gone until 5:00, when they come back to help their father prepare dinner. (Whew! That is one long, run-on fantasy.)

After dinner they clean the kitchen (to my satisfaction), we play a board game (with no fights over who gets the blue marker, the red die, or the last crumbs in an empty bag of Goldfish that someone *mistakenly* put back in the pantry), or we watch a movie (that we all agree on), or we sit by the firepit on the back deck and have a meaningful discussion that does not include the words *booger*, *fart*, *pinhead*, *lame-o*, *stinky-face*, *dork*, *party pooper*, *balls* (unless it pertains to a school-sanctioned sport), *snot-nosed*, *metal mouth*, *lazy-ass* (okay, that one's mine) or *e-tard*, which apparently is used to describe someone who can't figure out how to buy something off Amazon.com without ending up on a million different e-mail lists.

After that everyone puts themselves to bed so I can watch *The Daily Show with Jon Stewart* in peace, accompanied by my perfectly brewed herbal tea and one square of organic, dark chocolate.

I mean, honestly, is that asking too much?

Apparently it is, because by August I'm staring at the calendar again, counting down the days until school starts, at which time my fantasy changes to one where kids drive themselves to school even though they haven't graduated from middle school yet.

But all my summer vacation fantasies fade faster than a spray-on tan when I remember that since I work at home the reality of summer vacation for me is that *every day* is Take-Your-Children-to-Work Day. Trust me, that gets old fast. Even though I try to remain the responsible adult after school ends for the year, eventually (usually by the end of June) I loosen the reins during summer, just so I can get things done. For example, "Mom, can I stay up tonight and watch *Simpsons* reruns?" is not something I would even consider during the school year, but somehow it doesn't seem so bad in the summer when I know my son will sleep late the next day as a result. This means I'll be able to make phone calls in the morning uninterrupted, a huge luxury compared to the alternative, which is locking myself in the bathroom with my cell phone and speaking in hushed tones like I'm trying to buy decent cooking wine on the black market (hey, this *is* Utah, you know.)

Given all the negotiating that goes on around my house during summer vacation, I think both my sons will be ready to take the state bar exam before they graduate from high school. To illustrate my point, I give you this intellectual exchange that took place at our house a few years ago right after school got out.

"Mom, can I spend the night at Josh's house tomorrow night?" asked my eldest son, who was 12 at the time.

"No. I asked you to clean your room and you didn't do it." I responded, thinking that was the end of it.

"But that's a violation of my Constitutional rights." I looked at my dear child like he had suddenly sprouted a Siamese twin out of his left shoulder.

"Which? Having to clean your room, or not being

allowed to spend the night?"

"You never said *when* I had to clean my room, so technically, I'm not in violation." I have to stop letting this kid watch *Law & Order* reruns.

"When I ask you to do something I expect you to do it immediately. That's *Mom's* Law, which beats *Constitutional* law until you're 18."

"But I've never seen the Bill of *Mom* Rights, so how can you hold me to it?"

I thought about this for a second. "Fine. Next time I ask you to do something, I'll say when it needs to be done."

"So does that mean from now on *you'll* be punished every time you forget to include *when* in your request?"

"No, there's a little thing called double jeopardy, which means you can't punish a person more than once for the same crime."

"Is that Mom Law or Constitutional law?"

"Both."

"In that case, can I spend the night at Josh's tonight?"

"No, we've already been through that. You didn't clean your room."

"Which is why I can't spend the night at Josh's tomorrow night, but what about tonight? Double jeopardy, Mom."

Eighty-two days left until school starts. It's going to be a long summer.

My Mother's Day Breakfast

Yesterday (as I write this) was Mother's Day. I always wonder what will happen on Mother's Day because I have a husband who thinks leaving the toilet seat down constitutes a special gift, only to be given on special occasions—like Mother's Day. For cryin' out loud, we've been together for almost a quarter of a century. You'd think he'd get tired of fishing me out of the bowl when I fall in due to a miscalculated squat. If anything his absent-mindedness (for lack of a better word) has taught me to NEVER go to the bathroom in the dark.

Anyway, now that my boys are a teen and a tween, I want to make sure they understand that they MUST acknowledge all of the special occasions associated with the women in their lives, starting with me. That means on Christmas, my birthday, and, of course, Mother's Day, I'd better be opening a cute little box from some place like Nordstrom or the State Liquor Store before noon. (Okay, so that second one is only for after they turn 21. Until then they can get me something personal from Target if they haven't mowed enough lawns to shop at Nordstrom.) For their future womenfolk, those "*must remember*" occasions extend to Valentine's Day and any anniversary ranging from the day they said their *I-do*s to the first time they watched *Steel Magnolias* with their girlfriends and cried like babies (or whatever it is their gals choose to commemorate).

I can't stand it when mothers don't train their sons how to be thoughtful gift-givers. And yes, it has to be a learned skill when it comes to the Y chromosome. A male DOES NOT come out of the womb knowing that he should NOT give his woman a breadmaker for their anniversary just because *he* likes fresh-baked bread.

Ladies, you are not doing your sons any favors by making excuses when they forget to remember you on your special occasions. I don't care if Junior is off building Quonset huts for the Peace Corps in the jungles of Southeast Asia or sweeping mines in Iraq, there must be at least *one moment* on your birthday when he can put down the machete or the AK-47 and drop you an e-card. After all, you did change his diaper long after his friends were all potty-trained *and* you kept his fear of those yellow, *Have-a-Nice-Day* smiley faces a secret all these years.

Remember, you want your son to someday have a happy family life of his own. That isn't going to happen if he consistently forgets his wife's birthday, yet has the wherewithal to set the Tivo to record the annual *Jackass* marathon on Comedy Central. It's up to YOU to teach him to be a kind, considerate, thoughtful mate, preferably one who isn't afraid to educate himself on the investment benefits of fine jewelry.

So suffice it to say, my sons are works in progress. They aren't totally trained yet, but they're getting there. We've graduated from the macaroni bracelets that they made in preschool (and that I still wear proudly) to the onyx earrings and glass photo cube that they gave me yesterday for Mother's Day, both of which I love.

But the thing that really got to me this Mother's Day was that they (and their father) made breakfast for me. But not just any breakfast. No, they decided to make eggs Benedict. This might not seem like such a big deal, except that not one of the three of them knows how to boil an egg, let alone poach one. Now, I do admit this is my fault. I haven't been so good about keeping up on the cooking portion of their life-skills training (I can endure only so many enflamed oven mitts). However, kudos to them for getting out the *Betty Crocker Cookbook* and looking up eggs Benedict.

Sensing disaster, I decided to go take a shower.

When I came back, the kitchen was a mess, and I saw my husband using a spoon to ladle egg whites (along with some shells) out of a bowl, which was nearly impossible to do since the yolk had broken.

"What are you doing?" I asked.

"Separating an egg," he said with such intensity I thought he was teaching himself how to speak Japanese at the same time.

"Into what? Molecules?" I inquired. "Besides, you poach an egg *with* the egg white, so why are you trying to separate it?"

"This is for the Hollandaise sauce," my older son answered.

"You're making Hollandaise sauce from scratch?" I asked with the same shock I reserve for people who attempt to cross the Atlantic in a hot-air balloon.

"Well yeah," said my husband confidently. "Isn't that what goes on eggs Benedict?"

"Um, I'm going to go sort my underwear drawer. Let me know when it's time to eat." No one noticed when I disappeared from the kitchen.

About a half-hour later they called me for breakfast. The poached eggs were actually pretty good, but the Hollandaise sauce had the consistency of yellow lard.

"It was perfect a few minutes ago," my husband said.

"Yeah. It thickens up quickly," I replied. "But I'm sure

it'll still be good."

And it was. In fact, it was the best breakfast I've ever had in my life.

Afterwards, I asked my husband and sons why they didn't buy the packaged Hollandaise sauce. "You know, the stuff that you just add milk and butter to, and then ta-da! Instant Hollandaise sauce."

"They make that?" my boys asked.

"Uh…no," I said sincerely. "I'm joking, as usual."

Why bother with the truth when we were still all basking in the glow of a perfect Mother's Day breakfast?

Listen to Your Body

A female friend of mine recently asked me if I thought she should have a baby in the coming year (as if you could just push a button and get pregnant). She's about to turn 35 and feels like that bus is whizzing by. "I either need to get on, or let it go," she said wistfully.

"Self-imposed pressure is not a good reason to have a baby," I counseled her.

"Yeah, but I'm worried I'll hit 40 and my uterus will self-destruct," she replied. "I saw something about it on Dr. Phil."

I just recently read an article called "Listen to Your Body." It said that the healthiest time for a woman to have a child is when she's between the ages of 16 and 20. Can you believe that? Sixteen to 20? In what, gerbil years? When I was 16 I wasn't even smart enough to drive a stick shift, let alone raise a kid. Thankfully, I've matured since then. I can now drive a five-speed like nobody's business (just ask my 15-year-old son).

I refuse to listen to my body. I'm afraid of what I might hear. And sometimes it's loud enough for the guy next to me to hear, too. Over the years I've concluded that my body gives poor advice: I was 5'7" in the eighth grade, became nearsighted at 20, and by my thirty-second birthday had acne and gray hair. My hips blossomed when I was 13, but after two pregnancies and countless hormonal changes I'm still waiting for my breasts to develop. I think my body has a sick sense of humor.

I don't have to listen to my body to know I'm getting older. Not when the media constantly reminds me that saggy skin and wrinkles are akin to leprosy, and that our biological clocks are pitifully winding down like some old lady struggling to stay awake past Letterman's monologue just because the original members of Three Dog Night are his first guests.

And since we're on the topic, is that what I'm supposed to hear when I finally decide to listen to my body? A ticking clock? I broke down once and eavesdropped on myself. (I was all of 34 at the time.) All I heard was a low rumble (I think it was some bean dip I'd eaten earlier), but no ticking. Maybe my biological clock is digital, I thought. If so, I hope it has a snooze alarm. Even though I wasn't quite ready to pop out a litter of kids, I wasn't ready to give up on the idea yet, either.

Regardless of what anyone's body thinks, it's tough to decide if you should have a child. On the one hand, raising kids is a rewarding experience. You get to watch this tiny person miraculously go from a drooling blob to a self-sufficient adult (who, if you're lucky, has his own gas credit card and doesn't live in your basement). Using your experience and wisdom, you do your best to shape your child's personality into one that other people will grow to love and cherish as much as you do.

On the other hand, your offspring starts out as a crying baby with colic and poopy diapers, progresses to a whiny toddler whose favorite word is *mine*, and eventually becomes a teenager who demands an iPhone with an unlimited data plan and the keys to your Subaru Outback because even though it *is* a wagon, Lord knows the Mazda minivan is just too dorky to drive.

Before I decided to have kids, I knew in my heart that parenthood was not all Disney Channel and Hallmark cards (actually in retrospect it's been more like *Modern Family* and urban graffiti). To their credit, my parental friends didn't try to whitewash the travails of being a mom. (Well, actually I'm just being nice in case they read this. They lied more than Lindsey Lohan trying to pass a sobriety test.) But because actions speak louder than words, I *just knew* the reason people with kids relentlessly lobbied for their childless friends to have children is because misery loves company. Now I'm not saying having a baby is miserable (although I have to admit, the idea of becoming a schooner for some embryonic pirate for nine months didn't thrill me), but let's face it, everything about your life changes when you have kids. And even though all new parents will tell you those alterations are for the better, it's hard to believe this testimonial when it's given by a frustrated father as he mops up stains on the upholstery from a diaper blowout.

By the way, quick sidebar to impending parents—this diaper blowout phenomenon usually occurs:

A) In the back seat of the nicest, most expensive car you own, during rush hour on a freeway with no shoulder.

OR

B) At the end of the longest line at the grocery store with a cart full of ice cream, frozen fish sticks, and six pounds of perishable meats that can't be out of the freezer for any longer than it takes to check out and drive home.

OR

C) Just as you're ready to walk out the door to *the* fanciest soiree you've ever been invited to in your entire life—something along the lines of the Presidential Inaugural Ball or the Academy Awards. Is it merely a coincidence that your child explodes his digested lunch all over your new designer frock, which by the way cost more than your first car? I think not.

I'm particularly interested in how my businesswomen friends deal with the baby versus boardroom situation. These high-powered, successful women all waited until they were well into their thirties and beyond to have kids. But I've noticed that even these intelligent ladies go through a metamorphosis after they have that first child. They get all gushy and sentimental, as if *achieving* stretch marks constitutes a religious experience.

"Having a child is the most fulfilling thing you could ever do," coos one of my professional friends, as she sits on an inflatable doughnut waiting for her episiotomy to heal.

Another friend chimes in, "A baby creates a family, and suddenly life has meaning. All of the trivial things that consumed our time and money before—trips to the South of France, ski vacations, fancy parties, expensive restaurants, even just going to the movies or seeing a play—those things aren't important anymore." Of course, the new mom that's telling me this has developed a facial tick, talks to herself, and has a permanent array of multicolored baby bodily fluids smeared all over every piece of clothing she owns. Who am I to say that the trade-off isn't a good one?

Being one of these crazy women who took the plunge into parenthood, I must admit there are certain things that are definitely more fun when your kids are involved. The zoo, camping, birthdays, Disneyland, and Christmas all take on a new perspective. Watching your excited toddler, for example, see Mickey Mouse in person for the first time reinstates that sense of wonder you lost somewhere around your third career change or second divorce. And when your anxious fifth-grader discretely cuddles next to you around a campfire because he just heard a weird noise in the woods, well, all of a sudden camping isn't such a hassle anymore.

Also I've noticed that some of my more fast-track, corporate ladder-climbing (a.k.a. pushy), stressed-out friends slow down their lives after they have children (myself included). No more working late at the office, business travel gets cut back, and things like long lines, traffic, and bills just aren't the big crises they used to be. One previously high-strung guy I know actually smiled his way through a tax audit. It is important to note, however, that in the previous year his third-grade son had successfully beaten cancer. There is no doubt that this guy will now have his priorities straight for the rest of his life.

So what's the secret here? Does the baby come with drugs (for the parents)? Or is this slaphappy attitude the result of lack of sleep? It's hard to explain, but I know from experience that it has a lot to do with things like wrapping gifts from Santa on Christmas Eve, or teaching a child how to ride a bike, or seeing your kid's face after he aces a test you helped him study for, or watching your child nail a sax solo in the school band. I guess you just have to be there.

All of which was absolutely no help to my 35-year-old friend. "You're just as brain dead as the rest of my friends with kids," she said. "All you do is talk in circles," which put her back at square one: confused, childless, indecisive, and getting older by the minute.

"Try listening to your body," I said.

"I did," she replied. "All I heard was this weird, growling in my tummy that faintly sounded like my mother's voice saying, 'I told you not to wait so long.'"

Hmm. I'm pretty sure that means she should either:

A) Try to get pregnant right away,

OR

B) Give up on the bean dip.

The Big Ugly

Anyone who's lived in the mountains has a story to tell. I'm not talking about the convoluted tale of how you ended up living at high altitude or how you survived the worst winter of your life just two weeks after getting here, but rather *the mountain story* you're reluctant to share because it's just too crazy to be believed.

If age has taught me anything, however, it's that "crazy" is a relative term. Over the years, friends have cautiously shared their mountain stories around warm candlelit dinner tables while snow swirled outside. It could be my imagination, but I swear the storm rages a little more angrily during these confessionals, as if the mountain gets steamed when her secrets are publicly discussed. Even though several bottles of wine are usually involved when these stories surface, they don't sound crazy to me.

And here's why.

Back in 1992, my husband George and I had lived on Lowell Avenue in Park City's Old Town for only a few years. In those days, Lowell was little more than a gravelly blacktop fire road dotted with just a few homes. Several lots on either side and below us were open fields, and in fact, we had a clear view of Park Avenue from our back deck (from which we used to watch the Fourth of July and Miner's Day parades).

Even though our house was immaculate when we bought it, we still felt the need to make a few changes. Luckily, George's dad (who was also named George) was the handiest branch on the family tree when it came to building things, a talent his son unfortunately did not inherit. But that was okay, because we loved having my in-laws visit from California, and helping with a remodel gave them reason to come often.

Plus, George's parents loved the snow. Before San Diego, they had lived in Detroit for decades. And now that they had a son living in a frigid climate, George's dad took pride in teaching his son winter survival techniques, which of course included the proper way to shovel snow. George was amused by this, since he thought snow removal was about as challenging as eating a cheese puff. And to make matters worse, George insisted on using a *high tech* shovel called "The Big Ugly."

Living up to its name, The Big Ugly had a Z-shaped

handle (instead of the usual straight one) with the idea being you'd get better leverage. George's dad thought this was insanely stupid and was convinced that The Big Ugly actually gave you back problems. He told his son repeatedly, "If you don't get yourself a decent snow shovel, then I will." So with this philosophical difference in common, George and his dad would spend hours taking turns clearing the driveway and back deck with The Big Ugly, each steadfastly trying to convince the other why this odd shovel would or wouldn't work. These were probably some of the best times they had together.

Then one Friday evening in February 1994, while George was in flight on his way home from a San Diego business trip, I got a call from George's brother. Without warning, George's dad had dropped dead on a dance floor with his wife by his side. Doctors later deemed it respiratory failure and said that he never even knew what hit him. He had been a lifelong smoker who had given up cigarettes in recent years, but by then it was probably too late. He was 72.

When George got home that night, I told him about his dad. He looked at me stoically, like I was lying. "I just had dinner with my parents last night," he whispered. I remained silent because I didn't know what to say. He put on his coat, went out back, and aggressively attacked the snow with The Big Ugly.

Everyone deals with grief in his or her own way, so I

wasn't put off when George ignored me as I tried to talk to him while he shoveled snow. His emotional distance made it quite clear that he wanted to be left alone. I finally gave up and went back inside. But I couldn't bring myself to let him face his pain single-handedly, so I opened a second story window and helplessly watched over him as the scraping shovel drowned out his faint sobs.

Early the next morning, George flew back to San Diego, still disconnected from anything but his own relentless sorrow. I stayed behind to tie up loose ends, with the plan to fly out later in the week. During the night, snow dumped *again,* and by the time George left for the airport the drifts in our yard looked like a new mountain range.

Feeling alone and useless, I went out back to clear the deck. As I pulled The Big Ugly from its resting place, I saw that the plastic shovel blade had a huge crack where it attached to the handle. With the first scoop of snow, the shovel blade broke off, leaving a hopeless hunk of crooked metal in my hands. I couldn't believe it. The Big Ugly was dead.

Frustrated beyond belief, I hurled the shovel handle into the empty field behind me. It spun through the air like a demented boomerang and landed in eight feet of snow, never to be seen again. I started to cry, and for the next 10 minutes I stomped any remaining life out of that plastic shovel blade until it was an unrecognizable pile of rubble. Breathing hard, I felt both satisfaction and embarrassment at venting on a shovel. I quickly looked around to make sure there were no witnesses and was suddenly very melancholy when I realized how alone I really was.

I gathered up the shovel shards and carried them through the house to the garbage cans on the front porch. As I deposited the debris into the trash, it started to snow again. For some reason, I felt very defeated knowing I'd have to get to Albertson's before dark to buy a new snow shovel.

But then something weird happened. As I entered the house, an object fleetingly caught my eye. When I suddenly realized what it was, I froze. I slowly backed out the front door, and my intellect confirmed what I thought I had seen. There, leaning against the wall just to the left of the front door, was a brand new *straight-handled* snow shovel with a big red bow around it. No card, no note—just a shovel that had never been used.

I stared at the thing dumbfounded, briskly burning up brain cells trying to remember anything about a shovel being delivered. When I finally came up empty, thinking gave way to an unexplained wave of comfort, but my common sense still wouldn't let go. "Why would someone just *give* us a new shovel?" I thought. And then I shivered, not because I was outside without a coat, but because in my heart I knew the answer. My eyes welled up, and I tentatively poked the shovel to make sure it was real.

Immediately I got on the phone to everyone I knew in Utah and California, but no one laid claim to the shovel. I even had George's mom check their credit card statement to see if George's dad had ordered it. He hadn't (and George's mom knew nothing about it). After three hours of futile detective work, I went back to the front porch. The shovel was still there. I picked it up and, without removing the bow, used it to clear the driveway. With every scoop I felt a little better.

To this day we don't know where that shovel came from. I *do know* it didn't materialize from nothing, that a human being brought it to us, but I don't know what compelled him or her to do it. We hadn't lived in Park City that long, so we didn't know a lot of people. Our house was in the middle of nowhere, and our closest neighbor wasn't within earshot. And I know no one saw me stomp that shovel to death because I looked around afterward to make sure of it. Besides, they couldn't have put a shovel on the front porch that fast.

I've given up trying to figure it out. I think the quickest way to destroy the positive effects of a good mystery is to try to solve it. After you've lived at high altitude for a while, you eventually come to realize that not everything up here can be explained, nor should it be. If you can't accept that, then you need to go back to sea level. Personally, I'm comforted in knowing that this mountain I call home is the keeper of some of my best-kept, big, ugly secrets.

Made in the USA
Charleston, SC
10 July 2011